D1214332

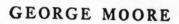

GEORGE MOORE

KENNIKAT PRESS SCHOLARLY REPRINTS

Ralph Adams Brown, Senior Editor

Series In

IRISH HISTORY AND CULTURE

Under the General Editorial Supervision of
Gilbert A. Cahill
Professor of History, State University of New York

GEORGE MOORE

BY

SUSAN L. MITCHELL

KENNIKAT PRESS
Port Washington, N. Y./London

GEORGE MOORE

First published in 1916
Reissued in 1970 by Kennikat Press
Library of Congress Catalog Card No: 70-102618
SBN 8046-0795-8

Manufactured by Taylor Publishing Company   Dallas, Texas

KENNIKAT SERIES IN IRISH HISTORY AND CULTURE

TO

"Æ" AND JOHN EGLINTON

WHO ALONE WERE TREATED MERCIFULLY
BY THE AUTHOR OF "AVE, SALVE AND VALE"
AND WHO ARE THEREFORE NOT LIKELY
TO BE INDIGNANT AT THE ASSOCIATION OF
THEIR NAMES WITH THIS STUDY OF
GEORGE MOORE

GEORGE MOORE

I

GEORGE MOORE might have cried with Walt Whitman : " Do I contradict myself ? Very well, I contradict myself. I contain multitudes." He has paraded before us unabashed, in a multitudinous personality ; ashamed of only one George Moore, the little Catholic boy of that name who went to confession. Yet why should he whose whole life has been spent in making confessions object to confession ? Perhaps it was the privacy of the confessional that affronted him, that so much good copy should be wasted, poured into the ears of unliterary priests, whose lips were sealed and unable to retail all that valuable material. Of course as a literary man he would deny the Catholic George Moore, and as I do not desire to wound him I will not refer any more to this child who was so likely a father to the man we know ; no need to when we have Moore the pagan, Moore the Protestant, Moore the artist, Moore the realist, Moore the stylist, Moore the patriot, Moore the anti-Irishman, Moore the dramatist : all personalities which he himself has revealed to us in the most enchanting fiction. I will come to each of these personalities in turn, but I shall begin with the only one of which he himself is not the creator, the George Moore, minted in Mayo, stamped somewhere towards the middle of the last century with an unmistakable Irish birthright which he has never been able to obliterate.

I have had great difficulty in collecting any facts about this George Moore, principally because the Celt is averse from facts, and when I enquired certain things of those who knew him intimately, I was swept off my feet by a torrent of opinions. Mr. Moore has always been a troubler of the waters of opinion. Even in the matter of his age the records do not help us. Doubtless the gods who predestined him to immortality saw to it that his beginnings were shrouded from the measurements of time. Computing by the light of mere mortality, we find recorded in " Who's Who " that his first published work, " Poems of Passion," appeared in 1878. As he must at least have known how to read when these appeared, there is something to be said for dating his birth from the early fifties, and we will proceed on that assumption.

George Moore, then, was born perhaps in

1852, the eldest son of George Henry Moore, of Moore Hall, in the county of Mayo, in the province of Connaught in Ireland. George Henry Moore was a distinguished Irishman, and his life has been ably written by his son, Colonel Maurice Moore. He might be said to have been the founder of the Independent Party in Irish politics, but his political intelligence undoubtedly did not descend to his son George.

George Moore, who describes with such fidelity of detail the personal appearance of the characters in his novels, should delight in seeing himself portrayed by another artist, and as this chapter purports to deal with the outer George Moore, I will recall my own first impressions. It was my lot to be living in London when what calls itself the Irish revival was surging there, for we must not forget that London was the source of that upsetting wave which draggled all our crisp young feathers. To me, shortsighted from my obscurity in midland Ireland, the greatness of London was not in its literary persons but in the city itself. It submerged me, and I instinctively raised myself on the shoulders nearest me. It was doubtless luck for me that these shoulders belonged to such as the Yeats, Martyn, Moore, Lady Gregory, Ashe King, but at first I did not know my luck. I thought that these people were merely ornaments for the drawing-room ; afterwards I realised they were ornaments for the world.

I lived with the Yeats in Blenheim Road— and what a lovely book I shall write some day about that most companionable household.

To me the persons I met there were not at first either intellects or notabilities, they were mere society. After a little—being of a mind with our old friend Prince Arthur of the Tennysonian idyll—I " needs must love the highest " when I saw it, I recognised them and all their company for what they were. So it came to pass that though of small account myself, and not now even in the memory of most of these—I was free of a great company, and my mind, a little overawed by W. B. Yeats, Martyn and Lady Gregory and always inclined to levity, fastened itself on a name that seemed. to give a lightsome mood to whosoever mentioned it, and I grew curious about Moore. Yet when at the rehearsal of " Countess Cathleen " in some dark by-way of London, I was told he was present, I cannot recall any form, only an irritation in the dusty atmosphere. When next I met George Moore it was in my own city Dublin, where every brewer pleases and only literature is vile, but I, who still trailed some of the clouds of reverence that I brought with me from London, looked at this man of wicked books with an excitement that even irreverent Dublin could not damp. It occurred to me to wonder at what age Satan brands his votaries, as they told us in the Sunday-school books and as I still believed, because Moore, who everyone said was a very wicked man, had the rosy face and innocent yellow hair of young virtue, kindness was on his lips, though his eyes were not quite so kind, a little slow in following the lips. I had met in London another yellow-haired writer, but he was pale and pasty of complexion — and Moore was not like Symons. No, he was not like Symons; it counted in his favour. George Moore seemed to me then to be a man of middle height with an egg-shaped face and head, light yellow hair in perpetual revolt against the brush, a stout nose with thick nostrils, grey-green eyes, remarkable eyes, a mouth inclined to pettishness, lips thick in the middle as if a bee had stung them. He had champagne shoulders and a somewhat thick, ungainly figure, but he moved about a room with a grace which is not of Dublin drawing-rooms. Afterwards, seeing George Moore in the street, I found he was the only man in Dublin who walked fashionably. The strange word suits him; perhaps he is the last man of fashion in these islands. He wore an opera hat. Nobody in Dublin wears an opera hat, and, when Moore put it like a crown upon his yellow head or crushed it fashionably under his arm, it acted on Dublin like an incantation. I remember my own instantaneous homage.

This description I feel to be inadequate, and I have summoned to my aid the folklore of Dublin. Dublin is a crater of epithet, and whenever George Moore is mentioned out of the crater boil up such phrases as " an over-ripe gooseberry," " a great big intoxicated baby," " a satyr," " a boiled ghost," " a gosling." I am not satisfied with these descriptions, they are florid and untidy, and all descriptions suffer in comparison with Moore's own perfect etching of a portrait. He speaks in the latest of his prefaces of his " sloping shoulders and long female hands," with the feeling of a true artist. True there are painted portraits of George Moore. One by Miss Harrison in which she has set her own benevolence on her sitter's brow and her own candour in his eyes. It is not her portrait, however, which is most truly symbolic of Moore, but the famous portrait by Manet. In my (borrowed) copy of " Modern Painting," when I came across in the essay on Manet the words " He never painted anything that he did not make beautiful," I found them underlined by some waggish reader with a reference to the number of the page on which the reproduction of the Manet portrait appeared !

That portrait which is like nothing so much as the human symbol of a high-explosive shell.

George Moore's is a face dear to the caricaturist and in itself at times a caricature : the yellow hair, the fat features, the sly smile, the malice, the vanity. But as has been said to me, let someone begin to discuss an idea and in a moment the contours change, the fat shapelessness falls away, the jaw lengthens, the bones become visible, the eyes darken, the brows straighten, a hawk-like keenness is in the look. One does not caricature this Moore ; it is the face of the thinker, the man who handles ideas like a master. There is a duality in Moore that at once repels and fascinates and makes a study of him a delightful adventure in characterisation.

I am not a great reader and rarely read critically, but in my skimmings over fiction I cannot recall any writer so continuously implicated in his own work as George Moore. The creative mind, following the highest example, leaves its creatures once formed to fend for themselves. They are most close and cherished, an agony and a delight till they have taken shape and started on their own lives, then one feels them a part of one's self no more, they are separate beings. The child sets out to play his part in life. That is, perhaps, why the writer who most lays bare his soul in creation feels so little intimacy, so little modesty, when his thought confronts him later on the printed page. It is no more bone of his bone, but, lord of its own body, it has begun to form its own ties.

George Moore does not seem to me to create in this fashion. His production is more like that of the banyan tree whose own branches spring up into trees all round it, never detaching themselves from their parent, but in their many lives are one tree. George in his many books is but one George, he never loses sight of any of his selves in any of his works, but returns continually to write new prefaces to old books, re-animating in turn each of his dead memories. This is why I find it impossible to write of George Moore's works apart from George himself. Though I shall do my best as a conscientious writer to examine the writings severally, I know that I cannot hide from him in his banyan grove, he will spring at me from behind every one of his own saplings; although as a poet, in which character I shall first consider him, he has been more successful in concealing himself than in any other.

II

Mr. Moore, though never a penitent, has confessed himself so abundantly in all his work that his biographer's task should be an easy one. If we examine the matter closely, however, we shall see that while Rousseau, eminent among confessors, made confessions all about himself, Mr. Moore's are largely about his friends. As a poet, however, Mr. Moore presents few difficulties. It is easy to understand how a young man, heady with vanity and conscious of some literary power, should first seek in verse a medium of expression. He himself said once : " Every young man of literary talent has one volume of poems in him when he is young; the test of a poet is whether he can still write poems when he is fifty ! " Judged by this his own standard, Mr. Moore is not a poet. He published two volumes of poetry, " Flowers of Passion " in 1878, and " Pagan Poems " in 1881. In neither of these is there much more than competent versifying. They are wanting in that sincerity which is in nearly all his prose ; they are artful and more than a trifle perverse. But for this latter quality they might have

been written by any of those beneficed and
leisured clergymen whose elegantly bound
volumes of classically flavoured verse are
in so many eighteenth-century book collec-
tions. The patient cataloguer knows them
well, and knowing, yawns. In perhaps only
two poems of Mr. Moore's, "Ode to a Dead
Body" and "The Beggar Girl," is there a
hint of that sympathy which afterwards,
when he had found his real mode of expression as a novelist, made "Esther Waters"
the best of all his novels.

Mr. Moore is so interesting to a biographer
as a human being, as a novelist and as a
critic, why should I make any bones of dis-
missing his claims as a poet? A story I
have been told of Mr. Moore's boyhood
makes an appropriate comment on his
verse. He chose as a treat for his tenth
birthday to be dressed up to resemble a
Greek of Syria. With an ornamental sword
and mounted on a grey pony with Eastern
trappings he was led around his father's
demesne to the wonder of the peasants.
His love of "dressing up" made him write
verse as it made him study painting.

It will not surprise anybody who has
read Mr. Moore's verse to learn that his
favourite poets are Shelley and Swinburne.
His two volumes are a whole whispering
gallery full of echoes. It is amazing to see
a man who began by so servile an imitation

18

of other men develop the astonishing originality of " Ave, Salve and Vale."

As well as these two volumes of poems, Mr. Moore collaborated with a friend in " Martin Luther," a tragedy in blank verse. I have been told that a literary friend in Dublin once asked him about " Martin Luther." He instantly sprang from his chair and clutching his flaxen locks walked frantically about his room wailing : " What have I ever done to you that you should remind me of this thing ? " It is so difficult to get a copy of this work to-day that I am tempted to believe Mr. Moore bought up the copies himself and destroyed them.

Every now and then when he was in Dublin Mr. Moore would discover a new poet and try him on the stony silence of John Eglinton. His faith in Swinburne was somewhat shaken by the steady refusal of the Irish school of poets to see more in him than eloquent emptiness. " Flowers of Passion," however, fetches up to £8 from collectors, and will continue to go up in price no doubt, in spite of this chapter.

III

Nobody in Ireland has ever seen any of Mr. Moore's paintings except "Æ," to whom he once shyly showed a head, remarking that it had some "quality." "Æ" remained silent.

IV

WHEN I come to speak of Mr. Moore as a critic I have nothing but my mother wit to guide me. As to the intrinsic value of his criticism, I have not the knowledge which would enable me to gauge it. This defect of mine has always been a great trouble to me, though Mr. Balfour wrote encouraging words to such as I when, after profound examination into the question of criteria, he decided there were none save personal preference. Should I be timid in following where so intrepid a thinker has led the way ?

Mr. Moore wrote " Impressions and Opinions " in 1890, and " Modern Painting " in 1893. To many people these books of criticism are by far the most interesting of his work. He has a great deal to say about writing and painting and he is so interested in both these arts that he compels our interest. He knows why he likes a painter or a writer and he tells us why with all the skill of language he possesses. Nobody does this quite in Mr. Moore's way, because very few people bring such a momentum of personality to bear upon their writing. At the moment I can think of no writer about writers to compare him with, except Chesterton, and I am aware that it is an unfair comparison and exposes at once the lack in Mr. Moore's writing. Mr. Chesterton is indeed a shower of star dust rather than a star, yet if that shining dust of epigram had an organic unity he might be one of the great writers of the world. He has been brushed by the wing of genius, and Mr. Moore, whose altars are never cold—for he has made many a burnt offering—has never been able to lure the winged ones his way

Yet his art as a writer is a genuine art. But while his writing about writers is always very interesting, his writing about painting is a different and a greater thing. I explain it to myself this way. He married his art as a writer and settled down comfortably enough beside her for life, he will never leave her, he would be lost without her. Painting he loved, but did not marry. It was an unrequited love. All the ardour of his youth went out to her. He worked hard in her service but she would have none of him. All he knows of romance is on that side of his nature. This warms us as we read his "Modern Painting." We know as he writes about painting that his adoring eye is still on the palette which will never do his bidding. He loved those colours, he knew all they could do for others but they never glowed for him. Hence every sentence he writes about pictures he rolls upon his tongue, it is a sweet morsel, and he gives us with full justice every particle of its flavour. That one should smell the paint in these sentences is not wonderful. Someone told me that Mr. Moore said he loved the smell of oil paint better than the smell of flowers. Where one disagrees with Mr. Moore's criticism—and who agrees with anyone's criticism?—is perhaps, as has been said to me, because he cares more for art than nature and for painting than for art.

"Impressions and Opinions" are very much Moore weighted with all his sincere and unreasonable personality; serious and reverent as in the Balzac article where he helps us to look just for an instant into that million-peopled brain; in the impressions of Turgenieff, Verlaine, Zola, the Two Unknown Poets, full of as keen a scent for literature as the foxhound for the fox. That he does not always "kill" is part of the charm of our Moore as a critic, he allows himself to be deflected from his object as in the Zola article by a very deliberate ill-temper, and in the Turgenieff article by the pettishness that makes him sell his Dostoevsky for a foolish epigram. In "Mummer Worship" he enjoys himself, as we all do when dignifying our personal antipathies by the name of opinions we give our public "a piece of our mind." The articles on "the *Salon Julien*" and "Degas," the "Rencontre in a *Salon*," "the New Pictures in the National Gallery" really should belong to "Modern Painting" and are as at home there as Moore himself in the company of oil tubes and easels.

It has been said to me of Mr. Moore that he had enough credulity to make him a bishop, but that he met Manet before he met Christ and that to Manet he has given all he knows of worship. However orchestrated his art criticism, however various the instruments he employs, whatsoever painters he writes about, one theme runs through all the essays—Manet. One doxology ends them all : "Glory be to Manet, to the most potent squeezer of the fat oil tube, to the last manufacturer of quality in oil painting."

And one understands it so well. Mr. Moore's romantic devotion to painting, his long effort to use colour, that real understanding and appreciation of what it could do that is most certainly revealed in every article he wrote about painting, and his pathetic failure to do anything he wanted with it ! No lover ever poured his unrequited love in sonnet with more passion than Mr. Moore in these essays has sung his unrequited love of oil paint ; this love that even affected his politics and made him a traitor to the reigning house in

England because they did not possess a
Manet among them. Manet could do all
things with paint. What a god! He calls
his essays, " Whistler," " Corot," " Ingres,"
" Chavannes," " Millet," " Monet," " De-
gas " ; he might have called them all
" Manet," so much do we surmise behind
all his great archetype. His " Modern
Painting," with its many essays, sings the
Benedicite Omnia Opera of the god Manet.

One suspects that he did not jump into
this worship of Manet all at once, but that
his love for the unpopular Manet was a
reaction from a love of some popular painter
like Doré. His ardour is that of the convert.
I have been converted and I know.

That Mr. Moore's art criticism has a
devastating quality at times is illustrated
in his " Modern Painting " by the article
on the Victorian Exhibition. It is not so
much a consideration of the art as the
explosion of a mine under it. In conversation this devastating quality was happily
illustrated when he visited a friend who had
an immense picture by Sargent of three
ladies seated amid high-class furniture. It
was hung in the dining-room, but during
dinner George never lifted his eyes to look
at it. " You have not looked at my Sargent,
Mr. Moore," his hostess at last said. " No,"
said George, " I was afraid you would speak
about it. I don't like it. But I have just

been talking to somebody who saw it at the Academy and who admires it tremendously." " Would he like to come here and see it again ? " asked his hostess. " No, I don't think you would like him to come," said Moore. " You see, he is my greengrocer. He likes pictures and he talks about them to me when I go to pay my bills. ' Oh, Mr. Moore,' he said, ' wasn't it a beautiful picture ? Here were the young ladies on the sofa and you knew the footmen were on the stairs handing up the young gentlemen, and they were drinking champagne all day long. It was real high life.' And that is exactly what I think of the picture," concluded George; " it's just the greengrocer's idea of high life."

Mr. Moore's genuine love for art was the tie that bound him to many strange associates ; it was the basis of his love for Shelley, his admiration of Yeats and " Æ." It was John Eglinton's grace in turning a sentence that secured him the friendship of Moore, and even in the shearing of Edward Martyn, conducted with all the ferocity of a near relative, the wind was tempered by Moore's respect for Martyn's very real dramatic talent. Indeed, so great is Mr. Moore's love for art that I believe if when he returned to Ireland he had found good stained glass in the Catholic churches, and altar pieces there by artists he respected, he would have become an ardent champion of the Catholic faith, and Protestantism would never have received an adherent so little to her mind, and whose hunger for art she also was totally unable to satisfy. For I can never believe that it was the parish priest's love of a good dinner that drove Mr. Moore from that fold, such a love is not really alien to Mr. Moore's nature and could be no stumbling-block to his faith. So desirable and human a characteristic might well have won his praise, if to the love of a good dinner the parish priest had united love for a good picture.

V

WOMEN, I feel, are only intermittently self-conscious and the business of putting together the wisdom obtained in these momentary glimpses of themselves is a troublesome one, because they live only occasionally in their minds at all. Therefore no woman has risen up to write a book containing the whole wisdom of woman, and I for one pray that such an one may never arise to profane our mysteries. For the most part we look to men to reveal us to ourselves. Man is our *logos*, articulate on our behalf. Women are, I think, curious, prying creatures, seeking mind. I can easily explain to myself Mr. Moore's ideas about women and why they are not so offensive to women as to men. There is often a wreckage of women about the lives of prominent writers or thinkers or any men who stand above their fellows. They attract women as the lighthouse attracts the birds, and the wheeling creatures die of exhaustion, unable to reach the light and unable to leave it. Mr. Moore, perhaps, makes the common error that it was his person and not the light they fancied on his brow that lured them. Therefore perhaps

he and they are quits. The sexes perhaps
are always quits, and when Mr. Moore says
such and such a one was or was not his
lover, we women are unmoved. We think
he is rather an idiot to talk so much about
it, and we can only comprehend vicariously
and through our sympathy with them the
tremendous to do men raise over Mr.
Moore's breach of their convention. We
make him a present most cheerfully of any
little pleasure he gets out of fancying we
are in love with him while we crane eagerly
over his shoulder to read what he writes
about us. His main theme in his novels is
love. What are " Evelyn Innes " and " Sister
Teresa " but the only novels exclusively
about love in the language ? Funny person.
Women know instinctively all he knows
about love and more also. It is intellect
we are after. The intellect he brings to
bear upon love we wash out of his novels as
carefully as the miner washes the gold from
the clay.

In Mr. Moore's continual occupation with
love and lovers I find him less unpleasant
than many of the English novelists. There
is a less adhesive quality in his coarseness,
and I think it is because he has never been
able even to simulate passion. His nature is
strongly biassed in one direction, but his
intellect has balanced him : there is a cold
quality in it. Passion would, perhaps, have

spared us his tiresome preoccupation with what one might call millinery and confectionery in the love adventures in his novels. But how absurd I am! Given passion, the novels would never have been written. In that grotesque character of his where mingles much that is noble with much that is base, I think that beauty has never had her lamp put out. It seems to me that the women in Mr. Moore's novels are such as no woman would ever draw aside her skirts from. He has not created a wholly unpleasant woman, and some of his women are delightful beings, docile to life, mother-hearted, full of wonder and trust, illimitably kind. We can recall Alice in " Muslin," Esther Waters, Kitty Hare, Agnes Lahens, Evelyn Innes. We are often suspicious that Mr. Moore was by nature an amiable and kindly gentleman, who ought never to have annoyed anybody, but either a false idea of art led him into evil courses or a natural impishness of temper, which no training could subdue. Nature never intended him to write droll tales like Balzac. He is not at home in them, and, when he does violence to our feelings, I suspect he does violence to his own. He brazens it out, of course, like the nasty little boy who puts out his tongue at one, and does it all the more, the more he thinks it annoys. Is there a little devil in Mr. Moore that makes him want to annoy ?

Most of us owned one in our early days, but grown-up obligations made us put the chain on him. Mr. Moore has never grown up and his little devil is an active little beast.

We expect this impishness in Mr. Moore annoys his men more than his women readers. There is hardly a naughty boy's trick which is new to us women ; we have laid the rod in pickle so very often. Mr. Bernard Shaw understands women much better than Mr. Moore, but we do not like our Bernard ; he sees too much with that chill grey eye of his. He would be good to us in actual life, clothe us and feed us and give us good wages, but what woman can forgive " Man and Superman " ? Mr. Moore in actual life would fly from all that was disagreeable in us, unless he could use it for literary purposes. It would not be agreeable to him to work at social problems like Mr. Shaw. But Mr. Moore pleases us more than Mr. Shaw. Mr. Moore often totally misreads us, but we do not want to be read, we want to read ; we do not want to be understood, we want to understand. And when Mr. Moore adopts, as he so often does, the Sultan attitude towards women, with its false air of petting and protection, we are not offended. We like, even those of us who do not wear it, to be told how men are subjugated by powder and paint. The more hardworking we are, the more we love to hear of those women whose only labour is that they may achieve an instant's beauty. Yet women are the sincerest creatures and but seldom taken in even by those false statements of life that they find so extremely comforting.

Mr. Moore once said that his brother Maurice was the only member of his family who knew how to behave as a gentleman. Well, Mr. Moore is an amazingly truthful person, and this commentary upon himself is illuminating in view of the liberties which in his later books he has taken with his friends. He has never had any private life himself, and he regards as eccentricity the objection his friends have to the private lives invented for them by him. In his essay on Corot, Mr. Moore tells how once he came upon the old man painting in the woods. After admiring his work, Mr. Moore said to him, "Master, what you are doing is very beautiful, but where is it ? " Corot flicked his brush in the direction of a clump of trees a couple of hundred yards away and said " There." Corot was improvising from a dim suggestion. He did not want to be too close, to lose grip of his subject in a mass of details. This story is a parable of Mr. Moore and his friends. He did not want to see them closely, knowledge of detail would have interfered with his picture. How important it was to him not to get too close to his subject, the following story illustrates : Last summer returning from Kilteragh in Sir Horace Plunkett's car, having lunched there and been treated as an honoured guest, he seemed penetrated by the kindness of Sir Horace. He said to me : " Why, Plunkett is a most intelligent man, he has a real intellect. I never spoke to him before. I never understood ' Æ's ' belief in him. ' Æ ' was right, he is never wrong. Why does Plunkett treat me like this after the way I wrote about him ? He must be a good man." Then, the first generous impulse past, he recurred to what really mattered—his writing, and with a sly smile said, " How fortunate it was I wrote my book before I knew him." Bouvard and Pecuchet were already fixed in their places, no intimate knowledge had come in time to spoil the literary effect. As I write this little story with a horrible exactness I cannot help feeling what an admirable gem of fiction it might have become in the capable hands of Mr. Moore. He would have got out of it the whole first volume of a novel.

Mr. Moore is no Rabelais, his Irish nature forbids him. He is no French novelist at home in his sins. I once was present at a social gathering in Dublin which tried to imitate what we have grown to believe—

it is probably fiction—was the life of the
Latin quarter in Paris. There was just one
person present who was native to that life
and at home in it, and he was not Irish.
The others! My goodness, how funny they
were! Dear things, they had never learned
how to be anything but good, and they
couldn't learn. They were as awkward as
dancing bears. Conscience sat on them like
Sunday clothes, the atmosphere was as
gloomy as a church heavy with mea culpas.
They drank pitifully, it was the only road
they knew to Verlaine. There may have been
a time in Ireland when your young blood
could carry his drink "like a gentleman."
Alas, I never saw it. When your clever
young Irishman rots his brains with drink,
they rot, that is all, and the decomposition
is a horror to fly from. Perhaps the Latin
races can sin gracefully, the Irish cannot.
And Mr. Moore's sinning? He cannot
escape from his birthright, Lough Cara set
her seal on him, "islands lying in misted
water, faint as dreams." As Silenus he is a
poor thing. His leer is so much " make-up,"
and it is the more revolting because he is
naturally sincere. He has no genius for the
gross. It is a creed with him not to be
ashamed, but here I catch him tripping,
for he is ashamed of being ashamed. Shame
would become him well who has so griev-
ously betrayed himself. When he speaks

in " Memoirs of My Dead Life " of the shock he experienced in a glimpse of his " ugly old face," I wish some mirror had showed him his ugly old soul! He cannot, however, entirely obscure his natural kindness. Many women must have found him a good friend. It is an artifice and a peculiarly irritating one that makes him so continually translate his kindly human feeling into terms consistent with his perverse literary theory.

VI

THOUGH levity is justifiable and even commendable when one deals with Mr. Moore as a poet or a painter, for one does not take him seriously in either of these aspects, it would be entirely out of place when one comes to speak of Mr. Moore as a novelist. Personally—and I need not apologise for personality in an intentionally personal book about a very personal writer—all Mr. Moore's novels are very distasteful to one who never feels quite comfortable or happy when obliged to voyage in fiction outside the safe harbourage of "The Wide Wide World," or "Mansfield Park." I have an ingrained propriety of mind that makes me most at home in a novel where the young lady marries the Rector, who should, if possible, be the next heir to a baronetcy ; and where all the characters walk daintily in the guarded paths of life. But I have been warned against the error of confounding my likings with my judgment, and while my personal self is most unhappy with the Balzacs, the Turgenieffs, the Flauberts, the Daudets, the Hardys and the Moores, my intellect is stimulated by such society. Like most women, I do not live in my intellect, but I derive great benefit from my occasional visits there, and when there and in the seat of judgment, I allow no personal predilection to influence an intellectual decision. My intellect, then, having examined all the evidence, assigns Mr. Moore his just place as a novelist. " Esther Waters " and " The Mummer's Wife" are masterpieces of the naturalistic school. With a more varied mind than Hardy, Moore has the same sub-human insight. It is the uncanny and instinctive underground knowledge of the domestic servant. It has the same minuteness, the same unemotional completeness. Had servants an intellectuality commensurate with this instinct what terrors we should experience ! But luckily for us they have for the most part a simplicity and warmth of nature which turns this sinister instinct into an engine for our comfort. While Mr. Moore in his "Ave, Salve and Vale" has turned it into an engine for the discomfort of his friends, in his other novels he has used it with great skill in an examination, pathologically minute, of the emotions. The ordinary novel reader is very like the ordinary theatre goer, both desire a sort of after-dinner lounge for the mind. It is most distressing to such persons to find themselves in a dissecting room where humanity is laid upon the table and that

interior life so happily hidden from the
un-intellectual man is exposed in all its
complicated workings. He feels it to be an
indecency, an outrage, though he may admit
its value. Dear ordinary person, I am entirely
with you in my prepossessions and tastes !

From the year 1883, when he published
" A Modern Lover," till to-day when he is
publishing his " Brook Kerith," Mr. Moore
has been incessantly busy writing. Naturally a lazy man, as those who know him
best assure us, he has compelled himself
to arduous mental labour. He has deserved
well of his art, he has propitiated it by the
sacrifice of many things dear to the ordinary
man, he has not even withheld his friends.
He has written unblushingly of many lovers,
but his art has been his one love all his
life, and he has been to her the most faithful
of devotees, and he has had his reward.
Three of his novels show us very clearly
what this reward has been. In " The Mummer's Wife " Mr. Moore obtained power, in
" Esther Waters " sureness, and in " Ave "
he found a complete expression of a most
vivid and original personality.

Mr. Moore in his " Confessions of a Young
Man," published in 1888, tells us the story
of his journeying from Mayo to Montmartre, of his life as an art student in Paris,
and of his return to London and his self-
imposed servitude there to the art of writing.

There is little to distinguish his story from that of other ardent young men of his day or of ours, except the determined publicity he gave it. I remember when I was a little schoolgirl pulling out a shaky tooth with a determination to let no pain deter me, because in five or ten minutes I should be able to show the tooth to my schoolmates and boast of my sufferings. Mr. Moore, with as many teeth as a crocodile, has pulled them all out in his " Confessions of a Young Man," and hasn't spared us a single reminiscent pang. This bad boy of English literature who does his own birching so persistently and publicly tells us of his selfishness, his folly and perverseness in Paris, and how he found that painting was unattainable for him, and how he had the sense to drop it and make another bid for fame. I do not regret his Paris, however, when I come to read his novels. How intolerable his realism would have been on an English foundation. If an Irish writer must travel, then I think the long way round by Paris is the shortest way home for him. Synge found it so, and James Stephens is travelling that way also. Paris saved Mr. Moore from the English idea that the novel is meant merely to amuse. In the English novels, with a few exceptions, one finds no light, no air, they treat of love as if it were one of the courses at dinner, a heavy dinner. Paris also may have saved Mr. Moore from building on this foundation because it influenced him in his ideas about women. However narrow his realism, however obsessed by sex, your French novelist does not seem to be able to get away from the conviction that woman stands for beauty. His belief is a fugitive gleam, perhaps, from some old pagan memory, flitting here and there across his darkness.

Moore in his " Mummer's Wife " is affected by the realists, but his Irish temperament saved him from what might easily have degenerated into a catalogue of details and the use of the observer's notebook. He gradually obtained mastery over his materials and his art became less a picture of life and more and more a manifestation of his own temperament. In " The Lake," written in 1905, for the first time he began to get a mastery of his style, long practice had brought him to the point where he deserved to be called a writer as distinct from a story-teller. We begin more and more after this book to find happy turns of phrase such as that which delights us in " Ave," when he speaks of Yeats' attempt at a joke being " lost in the folds of his style." " The Lake" was written in Ireland. It seems as if it was a true instinct that drew him to Ireland, his incessant labour for his own making was not in vain, his best work was done here.

VII

THE reviewer, that literary agitator, who could not live at all but for the strife he stirs up about writers, will say that my attempt at a criticism of Mr. Moore's novels is an absurdity, he will show me how it ought to be done. Even so, that is his business. I am attending to mine, which is to provide him with things to say. The writers will be on my side. They would surely rather that their books should be treated as living persons, first of all, than that I should show sentence by sentence how Mr. Moore or another learned to write them. This is the reason I provide for myself for choosing some of the most living to me of Mr. Moore's novels and showing the effect of their acquaintance on me, rather than writing in the usual manner of the reviewer of the effect of my acquaintance on them. Three of the writers who have preceded me in this series of "Irishmen of To-Day" have approached their task somewhat differently. Yet I cannot help feeling that Mr. Darrell Figgis, who so ostentatiously presents us with a clue to the labyrinth of "Æ," is lost in it himself and

can never lead us out. Mr. Hone, one of the
very few impartial Irish writers, is listless
about Mr. Yeats, his book has no more blood
in it than a balance sheet. There is blood in
Mr. Ervine's " Carson "; he knows nothing
about Sir Edward Carson, of course, but
his teeth are firmly fixed in the calf of
someone's leg, all the time, and he draws
blood without a doubt.

Mr. Moore in his preface to " Spring
Days," published in 1888, says that some
six years before he had noticed that " an
artificial and decadent society was represented by a restricted and conventional
literature of no relation with the moment
of which it chattered." He explains that
in spite of the great difficulties in his way
he had written " A Drama in Muslin " and
" A Mere Accident," " scorning all facile
success and walking to the best of my
strength in the way of Art." Mr. Moore has
certainly laboured in his realism in " Spring
Days," and alas! we labour in it too. A
human being will die who is obliged to re-
breathe the air he exhales and no other,
and these exhalations of our own lives, the
realistic novels, are heavy with death to
the imagination. Yet one cannot but acknowledge what a painstaking and faithful
picture " Spring Days " is of our middle-
class life, where no wild adventure occurs,
where crises come towards us insidiously

and not in the grand manner with a swoop
of wings. The nets of convention are about
us, character develops through a series of
little pushes this way and that. It is life,
but life repeated so faithfully that it asphyxi-
ates. I am glad Mr. Moore sloughed his
realism as he went on, though it fits in with
his nature that he should have revolted
against the insincere art of his day. It is
not easy for us now to realise what an up-
heaval these early realistic novels represented, and we are inclined to do them less
than justice. Mr. Moore struggled bravely
through the surf in these, they developed
his muscle as a writer, and through them
he learned to handle his boat " Esther
Waters " as a master mariner.

I read "The Mummer's Wife" when I
lived with the Yeats in Bedford Park, and
chiefly, with feminine perversity, because
W. B. Yeats had forbidden his sisters to
read it. I gulped guilty pages of it as I
went to bed of nights. Its merciless probing
into life intimidated me. I shrank from it
as the periwinkle from the pin. At this
distance of time I could not perhaps give a
very clear account of the story, but I will
agree with anybody that it is a powerful
novel; I was impaled on the point of it, and
I know. I have not the courage to read it
again. The fat actor who lures away the
poor little woman who becomes his wife lives

in my memory as one of the most real
human beings in English fiction. His relations with the woman he lured away and
the gradual deterioration of her character
are depicted with truth so merciless that the
most severe moralist could have added
nothing to the lesson it teaches. I understand that the book is regarded as immoral;
to me it appeared one of the most gloomy
moralities in literature. Mr. Moore is a
man who by personal preference would like
all love tales to end happily, but as an artist
and an Irishman he could not be sentimental, and he degraded the runaway wife
as if he had learned his doctrine of retribu-
tion in the plain black and white it would
have been taught him by any parish priest
in Connaught.

On Mr. Moore's return to his native land,
when I met him for the first time of speech,
remembering those tortured readings of
" The Mummer's Wife," as nobody was
within hearing at the moment, I asked
him, with the ignorant courage of my Puri-
tanism, why he wrote such horrible books.
He answered by asking me had I read any
of them. I faltered " No "—for I was
ashamed to confess to " The Mummer's
Wife." He said with that instant surrender
to attack so characteristic of him : " I
wrote one good book, 'Esther Waters.' I
will get you a copy of it." He went out of

the *Homestead* office and returned shortly
with a sixpenny copy of "Esther Waters,"
in which he wrote his name at my request.
I read the book, and my respect for him
grew great, for I thought I discovered in it
not only a brain but a heart, and in spite
of an extraordinary amount of evidence
since produced to me of Mr. Moore's want
of heart, I cannot rid myself of the conviction I felt when I read that book. To
this eager, inquisitive being who busied
himself so untiringly about life, and who
has lived a vicarious life of so much intensity
in the creatures of his imagination, I could
almost say when I follow him with heart-
ache through the story of Esther's sufferings, told with a most moving sympathy :
" For this thy sins be forgiven thee," as
the man in the audience at Fishamble Street
theatre cried to the sinful woman who sang
Handel's angel music at the first perform-
ance of the " Messiah."

"Esther Waters " is the story of a servant
girl, and in that lowly story Mr. Moore has
expressed the life of the lowly with a most
finished art and with real tenderness. In
" The Mummer's Wife " he shows us how
fiercely life treats the mere wisp of woman-
hood, without will, without character, who
is flung into its cruel currents—the fragility
that is her charm making her ruin the more
complete and the more tragic. In Esther

Waters we have a woman refined, delicate,
but in whom will and affection are so strong
that her character begins to grow from the
very moment when its destruction seemed
inevitable. Mr. Moore has an almost uncanny insight into a woman's being. In
" The Mummer's Wife " his analysis of the
emotions is so minute that one's sensibilities
are excited to a point that is quite painful.
In " Esther Waters " it is one's heart that
is touched. The following extract from the
preface to the cheap edition of the book
issued in 1899 shows us a Moore whom
perhaps many of his readers will not recog-
nise and whose acquaintance, I imagine, Mr.
Moore himself made with some surprise. He
says : " It was very generally assumed that
its (' Esther Waters' ') object was to agitate
for a law to prevent betting rather than to
exhibit the beauty of the simple heart and
to inculcate a love of goodness. The teaching of ' Esther Waters ' is as non-combative
as the Beatitudes. Betting may be an evil,
but what is evil is always uncertain, whereas
there can be no question that to refrain from
judging others, from despising the poor in
spirit and those who do not possess the
wealth of the world is certain virtue. That
all things that live are to be pitied is the
lesson that I learn from reading my book,
and that others may learn as much is my
hope." It was the first time in literature

that the life of a servant girl was treated with the sincerity of an artist. Mr. Moore had none of the desire to exhibit his Esther in the kind of picturesque way Dickens exhibits his characters. We can imagine Dickens, in spite of his humanity, reflecting : " How amusing these people are." Mr. Moore seems to say rather : " How alike everywhere is the human heart." He has no bias, he never patronises his servant. He does not look for the picturesque, but only traces the love of a mother for her child with a sincerity which, as I said before, was probably amazing to himself.

It is a curious matter this of the novelist; if one examined into it one would wander in dark labyrinths. If the novelist lives in his characters, who control him for the moment as the medium's body is controlled, and he receives vision through them and realises through them the purposes of life, will this imaginative life count anything to him who outside his writings—for all record we have of him—has just been a digestion and a breathing apparatus, a life so vicarious, that the wittiest woman in Dublin said of him : " Some men kiss and tell, Mr. Moore tells but doesn't kiss." Will there be anything chalked up to his credit in the tavern of life when he comes to drink again ? I leave it to you, my readers, I am no metaphysician. Here is a man, Moore, who has to many minds profaned his home, his parents, his most sacred ties, to whom writing is father, mother, home, lover, friend, life itself, who when he ceases to write will cease to live and will crumple up shapeless, nameless, mortal. What is there to him—any way—more than to a miner who sweats chunks out of the earth, who marries and leaves hearty children to perpetuate mining and the Iron Age of Man ?

In the year following the publication of " Esther Waters " Mr. Moore published " Celibates." It is written with great confidence and ease and shows Mr. Moore getting a grip of himself and his powers and possibilities as a writer. The morbid states it deals with are treated with none of the waywardness we are inclined to associate with Mr. Moore. The adventurer in life comes upon strange discoveries, and the novelist must be in a sense a pathologist of the emotions. It is when he goes beyond this and becomes the pathologist pure and simple that he nauseates us. Mr. Moore is too good an artist to make this mistake. He faces life as squarely as any writer I know, but one is in no danger of mistaking a page in any of his novels for a page in a medical journal ; a confusion of mind that one sometimes experiences in reading a modern novel. Mr. Moore's discoveries in life are not for the medical museum, but for the picture gallery. Mildred Lawson is a very clever study of a feminine George Moore — the same temperament with a woman's instinctive intellectuality, self-conscious but not profoundly so. John Norton is the voyager who hugs the shores of life; who has no confidence in his own nature; who is austere rather from timidity of temperament than from any moral self-consciousness. Mr. Moore has analysed him very ably. Agnes Lahens and Kitty Hare are snowflakes — exquisite, unsubstantial, reaching earth only to die.

" Celibates " is serious work, yet I find in it something that alienates. It opens up fields of speculation, and I delight in speculation where the mind takes wing, but such speculations as are here do not liberate the mind, they rather lead it into a blind alley. I am always inclined to take a book as a living creature, make friends with it or leave it alone as it attracts or repels. " Celibates " is one of Mr. Moore's books that I should leave alone.

" Memoirs of My Dead Life " is a book that attracts, and though there is much of the dead life resurrected in it that Mr. Moore would have done well to leave in its grave, for it has seen corruption and is unfit to be above ground —and much of it that should never have been born —there are some beautiful things in the book.

" Spring in London," " Marie Pellegrin," " A Remembrance," " A Waitress," " Resurgam," should not die. This is the Mr. Moore whom we know in " Esther Waters," who reveals himself partially in " The Lake," who is continually with us in " The Untilled Field," and of whom we have fitful glimpses in the waywardness of "Ave, Salve and Vale." The Moore who is neither a mock satyr, nor a nasty little schoolboy, but a thinker and a warm-hearted human being. This book is Mr. Moore's second essay in confessions, and while it is an advance on " The Confessions of a Young Man," showing greater power of selection and expression and less perversity and vanity—for life had no doubt been sitting heavily on Mr. Moore's head since those early days—it has not the fine originality, the wit and skill and malice and the entire indiscretion of the great Trilogy. Mr. Moore, who desires to pose before the world as the passionate lover, is quite unconvincing in this part. He is really interested in affection, and I think there are few writers who approach this subject with greater delicacy or fuller comprehension. The element of fantasy with which nature has endowed Mr. Moore began to appear for the first time in " Memoirs of My Dead Life," breaking out there as the heather does in a reclaimed field. How easy it would have been for this versatile artist to have been a writer of fantasies rather than a realist will appear from the following passage in "Resurgam." Perhaps he would have been a much greater writer if he could have mingled both moods together. We sigh for a little fantasy when we read the realistic novels, and Mr. Moore himself must have sighed for it also, for he finally broke away from naturalism and achieved a style in which his whole being could be reflected. He says in " Resurgam " : " Twenty priests had been engaged to sing a Mass, and whilst they chanted, my mind continued to roam, seeking the unattainable, seeking that which Raminese had been unable to find. Unexpectedly, at the very moment when the priest began to intone the Pater Noster, I thought of the deep sea as the only clean and holy receptacle for the vase containing my ashes. If it were dropped where the sea is deepest, it would not reach the bottom, but would hang suspended in dark moveless depths where only a few fishes range, in a cool, deep grave ' made without hands, in a world without stain,' surrounded by a lovely revel of Bacchanals, youths and maidens, and wild creatures from the woods, man in his primitive animality. But nothing lasts for ever. In some millions of years the sea will begin to wither, and the vase containing me will sink. My hope is that it will sink down to some secure foundation of rocks, to stand in the airless and waterless desert that the earth will then be. Raminese failed, but I shall succeed. Surrounded by dancing youths and maidens, my tomb shall stand on a high rock in the solitude of the extinct sea of an extinct planet. Millions of years will pass away, and the earth, after having lain dead for a long winter, as it does now for a few weeks under frost and snow, will, with all other revolving planets, become absorbed in the sun, and the sun itself will become absorbed in greater suns, Sirius and his like. In matters of grave moment, millions of years are but seconds; billions convey very little to our minds. At the end of, let us say, some billion years the ultimate moment towards which everything from the beginning has been moving will be reached; and from that moment the tide will begin to flow out again, and the eternal dispersal of things will begin again; suns will be scattered abroad, and in tremendous sunquakes planets will be thrown off; in loud earthquakes these planets will throw off moons. Millions of years will pass away, the earth will become cool, and out of the primal mud life will begin again in the shape of plants, then of fish, and then of animals. It is like madness, but is it madder than Christian doctrine? And I believe that, billions of years hence, I shall be sitting in the same room as I sit now,

writing the same lines as I am now writing :
I believe that again, a few years later, my
ashes will swing in the moveless and silent
depths of the Pacific ocean, and that the
same figures, the same nymphs and the same
fauns will dance around me again."

I cannot help feeling that in " Evelyn
Innes," published in 1898, Mr. Moore was
at a stagnant period in his development as
a writer. Perhaps he was ready for that
troubling of the waters that came to him
in the call to Ireland a little later. There is
everything in " Evelyn Innes " to make it
a fine novel ; an eternal idea—the struggle
of the spirit and the flesh—but the success
does not come off. This is, I think, because
Mr. Moore, while very fully assured about
the flesh, is diffident about the spirit, and
leaves us in the end undecided as to what in
Evelyn is fighting the affection of Sir Owen
Asher, an affection which seems to us a
more spiritual thing than the supposed
spiritual influence into which she is drawn.
Mr. Moore is not convincing in his Cardinal,
his Eminence does not satisfy us any more
than he does Mr. Moore, and above all he
does not satisfy Evelyn. His failure is Mr.
Moore's own failure, lack of spirituality.
Nevertheless " Evelyn Innes " will be for
many readers Mr. Moore's most popular
piece of work, and I hardly like to suggest
that this may be because it has some

touches which show Mr. Moore to have a sneaking regard for Ouida. I am not above this feeling myself. Is it not a little reminiscent of Ouida when Sir Owen Asher leads Evelyn through his hall on the evening of their flight to Paris? "Crossing the tessellated pavement through all the footmen, the majestic butler there solemn as an idol," "Owen bends over a marble table to scribble a note." Yes, and in Ouida's hands the pen would have been of gold with a handle of porphyry. I believe Owen Asher is the archetype on which Mr. Moore had fain fashioned himself. For his secondary hero Ulick Deane, he chose Mr. Yeats first, then tried to fit "Æ" into the part; afterwards rejecting both of these, he fixed on a hero who to our great sorrow was unknown to us in Dublin. The resemblance of Sir Owen Asher to Mr. Moore is very strong when in the scene where Owen learns that Evelyn has finally forsaken him for the Church, he roars and yells in agony in the presence of Ulick Deane and Merat the maid. I think, according to a Dublin legend, Mr. Moore behaved in much the same way when his cook spoiled an omelette!

All the same, I am touched by "Evelyn Innes," and I think all that is obscure in Mr. Moore's design in writing it explains itself in the last few pages of its companion book "Sister Teresa." Mr. Moore writes a

moving preface to the second edition of
" Sister Teresa," and in the story of the
unveiling of Frenhofer's picture, " confused
colour and incoherent form, and in one
corner a delicious foot, a living foot escaped
by a miracle from a slow progressive destruction," does Mr. Moore refer to those
last few pages ? I find it so, and the two
books gather a meaning for me in that scene
when Evelyn and Sir Owen meet in the
garden where the nightingales answer one
another. " Mute in the midst of that im-
mortal symphony about them "—a scene
that holds the nearest approach to spirituality in any of Mr. Moore's novels. What
woman will not be touched by a novel
where, as Mr. Moore says, " love is the
only motive " ? " A love story, the first
written in English for three hundred years."
There is a great deal of what I have called
the millinery and confectionery of love, no
doubt, but while this is a necessity to Mr.
Moore to supply his lack of passion, out of it
emerges affection, that quality in which, as
I noticed before, Mr. Moore is really interested, and which reaches us in these two
books through all their wearisome detail.

Mr. Moore republished last year his
" Drama in Muslin " under the name of
" Muslin " and fitted it with a preface—a
Georgian preface to an early Victorian novel.
It is a most unsuitable preface, but it is in

his later and better manner, the manner of " Ave." He threatens to become an eminent prefacer, an alarming threat. He has to some extent rewritten the book, and this makes it interesting to the student of his style. He can note pretty closely the commentary of the elderly George the stylist on the youthful George the story-teller.

Years ago in the west of Ireland, I was present at a prize-giving in a convent that I believe has some credit there as a place of education for girls. The Catholic Bishop of the diocese presided, and it was to me as if the solid ground had fissured beneath my feet revealing an underworld entirely unsuspected. In the narrow pride of my Ascendancy I had never dreamed of a Catholic Ireland that had its own presiding lawn sleeves, its own yards of white muslin billowing in restless rows, representing money that could be paid and was paid for teaching in French and the piano and the violin, all the very same trappings of education that I believed only to exist among the Ascendancy under whose shadow I was nurtured. And that these white forms represented young ladies who, when they dispersed from the convent, would each adorn a real home and a society that really existed behind the barriers of the R.M., the D.I., the Rector, the bankers and the county gentry ; a society with its grades and its codes of manners as strict as any I had known, this was surely an amazing thing. The whole solid ground of my experience trembled. How was it I had never glimpsed these muslin forms behind my Ascendancy barriers, never realised this excellent imitation of Society as I knew it ? Almost the same it seemed to be, a redder hand here and there perhaps, a heavier foot, but social and in the full swing of life ? The walled garden of the Ascendancy was no more to me a world, but a walled garden, and I another Eve, curious as the first. My inquisition was rewarded when I read " The Drama in Muslin." I had found my convent. It was on English soil no doubt, but its dispersed pupils went home to Ireland, and save that one takes for granted that they were not behind any social barriers there, as the muslin-frocked maidens of my earlier knowledge, how little different are they ! Always apart, preserving their hereditary characteristics as surely as the Jews. Mr. Moore's muslin girls play their parts in a drama of the Zenana, so thick is the purdah separating them from the strong boot and short skirt life in the south-western counties as my youth knew it in a decade or so after Mr. Moore.

Some decades have passed since then, with a breaking down of many barriers. I wonder if this generation of Protestants in the Irish provinces realises at all the social aloofness of the two religions in the days I write of, when in the west of Ireland a Catholic nurse might indeed hold a Protestant infant in her arms at the Protestant baptismal font, and hear our heresies unhindered, but a Protestant vestry could prevent the burial of a Catholic wife in the same grave as her Protestant husband, lest it might mar the perfection of a Protestant resurrection. The tables have turned on us now and we cannot complain, but are the barriers breaking down, is the fissure narrowing ?

I have lingered willingly over " Muslin," though to the critic my choice of this novel may seem an unintelligible fancy. I know my literary armour is not proof against attack, any bow drawn at a venture might hit me, so I fight my corner in my own way, following no rules but planting a blow wherever I can. "Muslin" is an Irish story, and I am writing of a man who is more characteristic of his nation than a Carson or a Redmond. In my writing I am like the child who suffers the meat course, but saves his appetite for the pudding. Moore the Irishman, Moore as we knew him in Dublin, is my pudding.

VIII

MR. MOORE is an Irishman. He was born in Mayo, where his family had been settled for several generations. He himself claims an English origin, but like Peter the Galilean, who, in spite of his accent, would have denied his province, the accent of Mr. Moore's mind bewrayeth him. And if one had no other evidence of his Irish origin, " Parnell and his Island," written with all the malignity of kinship, would have revealed it.

Everyone who writes about Ireland takes it for granted that it is a sick country, and each writer has his nostrum. I wonder are we really as sick as the doctors say, and shall I also in a page or so be advertising my potion ? Opinions are divided also as to the identity of the patient, and the question " What is an Irishman ? " causes almost as much concern as a lately debated problem " What is whiskey ? " Ireland is full of people all so busied in being Catholics and Protestants and Unionists and Nationalists that they have no time to betray any Irish character. Mr. Moore resisted the temptation common to every Irishman to obliterate himself in a movement, consequently his Irish character had a chance to emerge. But on those who have effaced their identity in religious or party nomenclature the question as to who is the real Irishman must continually obtrude itself. Can it be decided by religion, politics, lineage or name ? The little weeklies are often very fierce; mostly Catholic and Nationalist, it seems to me they would have these terms interchangeable ; to be Irish, they suggest one must be both. Hence the Nationalist and Catholic descendants of Cromwell's troopers with names unmistakably Saxon are accounted Irish, while such as I, a Protestant, having names stiff with Gaeldom in every generation of my family, have our claim to Ireland disallowed. Yet it is an old truism that for leaders Irish Nationality had Emmet, Tone, Fitzgerald, Mitchell, Davis, Parnell, all Protestants.

In Ireland a man's religion is not a personal and private matter, as in other countries it may be ; it is a public business, and the getting or not getting a job is involved in it. This being so, perhaps one should not drop one's eyes timidly when the subject of religion appears, but confront it boldly and examine into it. Boldly then I speak as a Protestant, and my Catholic friends shall hear a stiff-kneed Protestant confess. Irish Protestants have two inheritances: one is Foxe's " Book of Martyrs," the other is the history of their country. One tells of martyrdoms to Rome, the other of martyrdoms to England : the result being, in minds inclined to justice, a very cordial bias against both powers. The hounds of time had left us very little of Foxe but his brush; but England is ever with us, and those Protestants in Ireland who did not hate her for her treatment of their Gaelic ancestors were beginning to cultivate a very pretty exasperation with her treatment of themselves. One is often inclined to credit England with more brains than she possesses, and we may be wrong who imagine her policy is always to divide us in Ireland. She has sold this country so very often that we are either obliged to consider her diabolically clever or ourselves idiotically stupid, and of course the latter idea is a distasteful one. It was an old but always pleasant discovery to England that bishops are as a body pretty sure to be on the side of stability and safety and against violence, and in ruling Ireland through the Catholic bishops she secured safety from agrarian crime; but the fostering of a New Ascendancy brought about Hibernianism as the fostering of the Old brought Orangeism, and then came the Insurance Act, giving such a fillip to the Catholic Orangeman that the Protestant Orangeman who had become sleepy and indifferent began to feel stirrings of life again. The revival of his old sectarian doctrines in a Catholic translation brought the Orangeman to his feet. The sons of William rose, and while Joe Devlin, the Captain of the Hibernian team, kicked Ireland back one hundred years, Edward Carson, the Protestant Devlin, not to be outdone, with his Orangeman kicked her back a little further. And so it came to pass that the outbreak of a European war found one portion of Ireland organised, armed and drilled, and the other portion beginning to do likewise, and I for one can never make out whether this state of things was due to the Act of God or the King's enemies or to his friends the English Junkers who wanted recruits out of Ireland.

Is it any wonder that the inhabitant of a country such as ours, where so many creeds and parties clamour for a man's soul, cannot resist the temptation offered him of a comfortable pigeonhole retreat for it where it need never agitate him again? A country where it is more convenient to be anything rather than an Irishman. There are just two or three persons in Ireland who walk about freely unclaimed by any Shibboleth, and the tenants of the pigeonholes peer at them, some in admiration, some in fear, some in dislike.

When Mr. Moore came over to Ireland at

the time of the Boer War he was perhaps obeying his natural instinct as an Irishman : he was seeking his pigeonhole, and it is a proof of his strong individualism that in spite of the agonising desire to retreat there that he describes so graphically in " Ave," he resisted the temptation. Ten years of Ireland couldn't fetter him. Neither the Gaelic League, the Nationalists, the Catholics or the Protestants could detain this slippery customer, and he left Ireland with a gibe for them all, sparing only those amongst his friends whose independence of mind and indifference to his opinion perhaps protected them — " Æ," John Eglinton, and Oliver Gogarty.

It is very entertaining to read in " Ave " Mr. Moore's elaborate staging of his Irish career. It is not unusual for a man to see himself dramatically, but it is not given to every man to plan out a moving scenario for his life and then to make his actions fit it. I cannot help suspecting that Mr. Moore may have sketched out his " Ave, Salve and Vale " before ever he set foot in Dublin, and when he leaped upon the stage here all was prepared to his own order. But Mr. Moore, though a clever Irishman, was not, like so many others of his clever countrymen, clever enough to keep out of Ireland.

We in Ireland are gifted beyond most

peoples with a talent for acting, and in Dublin especially, while scorning culture, which indeed we have not got, we are possessed of a most futile and diverting cleverness. Mr. Moore's entrance on the stage in Dublin was marred by an audience having as much dramatic talent as he himself, and each so full of admiration for his own exercise of it that he had only a fierce criticism and no appreciation to give a rival player. We Irish are very much aware of our art as actors, we seldom lose ourselves in it, but Mr. Moore's dramatic concern with himself is so much inwoven in his nature that he can only be really himself in the various poses he assumes. He is absolutely sincere in each, and his Gaelic pose had for him a momentous importance that provoked the merriment of Dublin, where no one really believes in anything and where nothing matters at all save as providing a subject for conversation, and where if by chance a noble aspiration arises in some heart, the effect of its utterance is exploded in the percussion of a drawing-room jest.

For the cause of his failure in Ireland Mr. Moore, I think, sought everywhere but in the right quarter, the quarter I have indicated above. His discovery that Catholicism was to blame for all the futility of Ireland was a very diverting one to many people who never knew of Mr. Moore's Catholicism till he announced his Protestantism, and who thought his conception of the one religion as funny as his conception of the other. In pursuance of my resolution to wear no blinkers in this book, I am not afraid to state that I think the silence as regards discussion of their religious ideals between Catholics and Protestants is the most powerful cause of the cleavage between the creeds in this country. It leads to the most absurd misconceptions of each other's beliefs. I do not complain of any silence in the Press representing either side—goodness knows these have yelled loudly enough, and I think the Protestant has out-yelled the Catholic—I mean the silence of social intercourse, the absence of discussion. I speak as a fool perhaps, and my plea for discussion may be due to my own " absurd misconception " of the Catholic belief. The discussion of Catholicism with Irish Catholics —except in the ardent and early days of the Irish Church Missions—is considered among decent Protestants nowadays as a hitting below the belt. I can never be quite sure if this is because Catholicism in Ireland is reckoned among Protestants as largely the religion of the poor and as so ennobled by their sufferings for it that it is sacred from our criticism, or if deep down in the incurable Protestant mind there is not a persuasion that to Catholics must be extended the forbearance one gives to lunatics or children, poor things with whom no rational subject should be discussed and whose wildest statements should be allowed to pass unchallenged ; and that the shyness of Catholics in speaking to us of their religion proceeds from the fear of our laughter and of being led away by our superior wisdom. Where the first reason moves Protestants silence is right and just; Protestantism in Ireland has a bitter record and it does well to hold its tongue ; but to those who are neither poor nor unlearned, why offer the insult of our silence ? My panacea, as you may perceive, has at last been offered ; I cannot escape the common fate of a writer about Ireland. Free discussion is my potion. For God's sake let us discuss everything. So only shall we approach each other and learn respect for each other's point of view. Everyone knows the value of discussion in elucidating one's own cleverness and fixing one more firmly than ever in one's own opinion, and I have no doubt that free discussions between the religions in Ireland would be of more value to Catholicism here than much *motu proprio* and many *ne temere* decrees, for these it seems to me in another nation have paved the way to statutes like to *Præmunire*.

It may be that my little ripple of wisdom

will babble in vain against the Rock of
Peter, but it is in my nature to ripple on.
And as to Protestants, it was said. once of a
noble family in the west of Ireland, " You
will never get anything out of a Browne
unless you kick him first," and perhaps my
Protestants will respond to much kicking
and admit that their empty places of worship
bear witness to the fatal influence of pros-
perity upon a Christian Church, and will go
down on their knees and ask for the hastening of those Protestant Penal Laws that
some of us may feel are already overdue.

While I am not at all sure that the frankness of Mr. Moore the Catholic was not
without benefit to that religion in Ireland,
I am perfectly sure that a Protestant Mr.
Moore is badly needed to turn the hose-
pipe of his criticism on Protestant Ireland,
and if Mr. Moore feels sufficiently confirmed
in the faith to attempt it I invite him to the
task.

IX

In " Parnell and His Island " I find proof
of Mr. Moore's nationality as an Irishman,
because the contempt and scorn in it are
too bitter to be the work of an alien. The
gibe that we fling at an alien glances off
because our knowledge of him is seldom
intimate enough to point it, but when we
desire to wound our own people, knowing
the vulnerable spots, our shafts get home.
There is to me more indecency in " Parnell
and His Island " than in those of Mr.
Moore's books where this characteristic is
said to predominate. It is indecent in the
revolting display he makes of his country's
hurt. Aristophanes in Athens dared the
wrath of the Athenians when he satirised
their popular hero Cleon and himself took
the part of the character he satirised. That
is courage; if he had produced his play in
Sparta it would have been cowardice and a
treachery to his own city. What shall we
say of Mr. Moore who exhibits his country's
sores for the coppers of the Paris press, for
he wrote the book first for a French news-
paper. In all he has written about his
friends, all his indefensible association of

their names with events wholly fictitious, I
have never felt him so shameful as he is in
this book. Of course he never libelled me
in any of his work—and perhaps his fiction
had a certain art about it that blinded me
to its baseness and it was fiction. There is
no art in " Parnell and His Island," and
there is sufficient truth in it to make it a
horrible exhibition of Mr. Moore's own soul.
The writing is bad and immature, and Mr.
Moore's almost ludicrous haste to dissociate
himself from his country only implicates
him in it more hopelessly, because a mere
English settler, as he strives to represent
himself, would have felt none of the pain
that shrieks from every page of the book.
He would have had the contempt no doubt,
if he was made like Mr. Moore, but the pain
he would not have felt, nor if he had felt it
would it have reached us as through Mr.
Moore it reaches us. As an artist Mr.
Moore must thoroughly regret " Parnell and
His Island," and it is one of the books he
has never ventured to rewrite, though I
surmise black streams from it trickling
through others of his books. I do not dislike " Parnell and His Island " because in
it Mr. Moore traduces his country. Irishmen continually traduce their country and
sometimes as much by their praise as by
their blame, but because in this book he
identifies himself with her, though such

was not his intention, and the sharp edge of truth bites in this identity and it wounds, because there does exist such an Irishman as Mr. Moore proves himself to be here. I wish there was no such Irishman and that Mr. Moore had not had to pass this way on his journey to " The Untilled Field." Mr. Moore's mind has a continual tendency to nausea which spoils him as an artist. He writes contemptuously in " Ave " of the Irish that Douglas Hyde spoke, pouring as inky stuff out of his mouth, but Mr. Moore's pages are perpetually stained with the inky vomit of a mind incontinent. This may be salutary for Mr. Moore, but it is very unpleasant for his readers.

It seems a curious thing that a man like Mr. Moore, who in his early work disowned Ireland, should have been drawn to her later in life. We are not now even sure — eminent farewellist as he is — that he has really left her. It seems curious, but I find it quite natural. Hate is the other magnetic pole of love and draws its object towards it just as surely. Mr. Moore's hatred of Ireland polarised his thoughts towards Ireland and in the end he came here. Sometimes I fear that the hatred to England evinced by some of our journalists has so preoccupied minds that might have been of service to Ireland that it has caused them to educate their readers far more in England's concerns

than in those of their own nation. There
is no safety for a man in the practice of the
black magic of hatred. It binds him hand
and foot and leads him whither he would
not.

Mr. Moore's hatred of his native land is
responsible no doubt for that overturning of
his life that drew him thither. There is
much that is absurd in his own account of
his gradual divorce from a Mafficking London,
but there is also much that is pathetic. I
was living in London at that time myself,
and I remember the tin-pot heroics that
clanked side by side with real heroism. I
remember tawdry and tipsy processions,
headed by a whiskey bottle in Hammer-
smith Broadway, and the trays and baths
and tin trumpets wherewith respectable
suburban London signalised a British victory. I remember the raw boys, under-
sized, underfed, filling the departing trains,
the anguish, the fear, the shameful joys of
victory. England becoming self-conscious,
the tipsy bully lashing himself into what he
believed was a similitude of Elizabethan
greatness. It was very pitiful and very
human, and South Africa was very far away.
The London that I see to-day in the trough
of heavy seas is a very different place. It
has grown up suddenly and in company
with a grown-up England. The tipsy bully
was sobered in South Africa by the cold

water of many defeats. The final victory indeed was England's, but not until she had been taught a lesson by a handful of obscurantist farmers. To-day she is fighting a bully of her own size, it is a graver and a deadlier struggle, and it is at her own doors. England is anguished indeed, and the tea-tray and the bath heroics have passed away. A real heroism, I think, has taken their place, and some of the fineness of Elizabethan England has returned.

Mr. Moore's departure from England at the time of the Boer War was forced on him by a real loathing of London's attitude at that time and by as sincere a desire to stand by his country as was possible to his wayward heart. I have said many harsh things of Mr. Moore, though never anything so bad as he has said of himself, but the interior sincerity that prompted his return to Ireland I have never doubted, however I may have chuckled at his staging of the part he played here.

X

PERHAPS one might say that " The Untilled
Field " was Mr. Moore's indemnity to Ireland for " Parnell and His Island." I often
wonder if it was his own nature that took
him by the hand and showed him the Ireland that we find in this book, or did a
friendly finger, " Æ's " or Turgenieff's, un-
seal his darkened eyes. I can realise perfectly what Mr. Moore felt when he came to
Dublin and found himself in a town that,
even when it had heard of them, cared
nothing for Manet, for Balzac, for Turgenieff,
for French poets however exquisite; that
recked naught of the differences between
turbot and halibut and hake, or the sauces
which should or should not accompany
these; a people to whom all Moores were
equal, him of the Melodies and him of the
Almanac, and to whom Frankfort was as
great as George. Yet a puzzling people,
because though they cared nothing for culture, and ate but never dined, were yet so
nimble of wit, so polished of tongue, that
they could not be passed over as of no
account. A people from whom he felt
absolutely divergent in all matters of taste

and yet with whom he had ties of temperament stronger than in either of the countries where he had sojourned. The Ireland Mr. Moore knew in his early days was all a confusion to him, and detestable because his crude and immature art could not cope with it. We always detest what we desire to mould and yet cannot bend to our purpose. Out of that detestation he wrote " Parnell and His Island." But the Mr. Moore who found himself in Ireland at the time of the Boer War, had matured and was achieving his literary style. He heard all round him, amongst people whose lack of culture he despised, brilliant and witty conversation. He heard Yeats and " Æ " and Hughes and John Eglinton and Gill all talking the most excellent copy, and in high good humour at the discovery of so rich a soil he sat down and wrote the best-natured book he ever wrote about Ireland, " The Untilled Field." He felt no doubt that Ireland could be made productive of much good literature for him if he only tilled it. Alas, he did not realise that mental tillage had gone out of fashion here and that our intellect is all laid down in grass.

Mr. Moore's passion for re-writing led him somewhat astray in " The Untilled Field." The first edition had a spontaneity and simplicity that are sometimes lost in the latest one. The reader is vexed by the dragging into the text of a number of Mr. Moore's favourite perversities. One recognises them so well now, and they serve no earthly purpose but to irritate the reader and break up the form of an earlier and clearer narrative. The charm of the " Wild Goose " was a delicate thing which the last edition of " The Untilled Field " has shattered. I am all against this continual re-writing of books. Re-write by all means again and again while the book is in the process of making, but do not return to a book after years and think to recapture the mood in which it was written. When we pull the structure to pieces something essential escapes, something that was enclosed within the walls in the first building. I think Mr. Moore became infected by Mr. W. B. Yeats' passion for altering his work. In Mr. Moore's earlier work he was more occupied with the substance than the form, but in his later the form tends to master him. The effect on the reader of all this re-writing is that he begins to doubt the author's inspiration and to believe that he did not really know what he wanted to say. That definite imagination which is the most precious thing in any writer's work and which alone gives it authenticity, becomes blurred and one begins to suspect the fumbler.

The preface to the last edition of " The Untilled Field " is an entertaining fantasy.

Mr. Moore claims that Synge got from reading " The Untilled Field " the inspiration which drew him out of what Mr. Moore calls the " board-school English " of his earlier work into the living speech of the plays. I am afraid there are few critics of Synge who will take this view. It is well known to every student of Irish literature that Douglas Hyde was the true begetter of the rich dialect based upon a foundation of Gaelic idiom, and anybody can prove this who will turn to Douglas Hyde's rendering in English of the " Love Songs of Connacht " and the " Commentary." These appeared long before either Lady Gregory or Synge had loomed upon the literary horizon. Hyde was the first who, knowing Gaelic thoroughly, was able to discern the bony Gaelic structure underlying the Anglo-Irish speech, and Synge and Lady Gregory, who both had some knowledge of Gaelic, were able to follow where Hyde pointed out the way.

The Mr. Moore in " The Untilled Field " begins to be a more likeable person than the novelist and critic we knew heretofore. He devotes as much of his intelligence as he can spare from the development of his art to a sympathetic study of Ireland and her problems. Father McTurnan, Father Maguire, Peter O'Shane, Biddy McHale are not cosmopolitan but Irish characters. " The Win-

dow " is, I think, one of the most poignant
things Mr. Moore has written. The tales in
" The Untilled Field " seem to me to be
less art for art's sake, or even art for Moore's
sake, than art for life's sake, yet they failed
to impress Dublin. Many of them were
translated into Irish, but the Gaelic League
never seemed to cotton to Mr. Moore, and
we doubt if " The Untilled Field " as a text-
book ever enjoyed the popularity accorded
to the manual that instructed our young
Gaelic enthusiasm to " Put the butter on
the floor " or recorded the unnatural thirst
of " Art " who went so often to the well.
Among Mr. Moore's circle in Dublin it
awakened a certain nervousness, for Mr.
Moore was quite manifestly using up his
friends for copy, and one looked askance at
another and wondered how much was au-
thentic in the personal adventures attributed
to the characters in the book. Mr. Moore's
friends were to become better instructed as
to their function in his literature later on.

" The Lake," published in 1905, is memorable because it marks, I think, a change in
Mr. Moore as a writer. He had found his
style and from " The Lake " onwards he
handles it with great ease. There is some
beautiful writing in " The Lake," and the
book is a feat of construction because Mr.
Moore has contrived to make a novel of
some hundreds of pages out of the medita-

tions of one man walking up and down beside his lake and with but one idea in his mind. Mr. Moore is independent in " The Lake " of any of that paraphernalia of varied character on which the novelist usually depends. But the book is, after all, a *tour de force*. The meditation of the priest is a personal struggle and has little spiritual depth or intensity. There is in the book more technical merit of writing and construction than there is profound observation of life. The name of the priest, " Oliver Gogarty," is taken wholesale from a well-known Dublin doctor, and when the bearer of the name remonstrated with Mr. Moore, Mr. Moore replied : " Where can I get a name so good ? " In one sense the book is symbolical if not prophetic, for was it not about the time of its publication that Mr. Moore was preparing to shed the last rags of his Catholicism and appear as a naked Protestant before an entirely unmoved Dublin ?

XI

MR. MOORE has summed up in " Ave, Salve
and Vale " his Irish experiences, and I pro-
pose in these chapters to sum up our experiences in Ireland of Mr. Moore. In this now
famous Trilogy Mr. Moore invented and per-
fected a strikingly original form of the novel.
It was nothing new for a novelist to use his
friends as models, and the circumstances of
his own life and of theirs as a framework for
his story. But he was often shy about it,
and disguised and varied circumstance and
actor to hide identities. It remained for
Mr. Moore, who has never put on his clothes
since the day when as a little boy in Stephen's
Green he took them all off and ran naked
to the scandal of his nurse, to do away
once for all with subterfuge in fiction.
" The Untilled Field " made his friends
somewhat nervous, but no names were
named. In " The Lake " Oliver Gogarty's
name lent piquancy to Mr. Moore's hero.
It was a sort of trial trip in nomenclature,
and its success encouraged Mr. Moore to
come boldly into the open in " Ave " and
attach names to their rightful owners, and
use both names and owners for the purposes

of fiction with a complete disregard for the
feelings of the proprietors, marvelling only
that his friends should prefer immortality
in any other form than that he had chosen
for them. And no doubt success justified
him, for though some of his friends who up
to this had given him a fool's pardon for his
many breaches of faith and manners, were
deeply wounded by the Trilogy, the rest of
the world were amused and interested by
this new and daring form of the novel. It
opens up a horrible vista, if this method of
writing novels with real characters all under
their own names should become fashionable,
and people should even grow so depraved that
they would actually desire to be in such
novels, and it may come at last to this, that
we shall find the fashionable portrait painter
in literature as well as in art. Sir Edwin
and Lady Angelina will go to the fashionable portrait-painter in literature and say :
"We understand your terms for making a portrait novel of the happiest period of our lives,
for an edition we can distribute to our friends,
are £500. We have kept our love-letters, and,"
says Sir Edwin, "I have made notes on my
disappointed rivals, their lives and habits,"
while Lady Angelina slyly slips into the
painter's hand her notes on the girl who
wanted to marry Sir Edwin, and all her little
cackling ways. The Yellow Journalism of
America, with its shameless inquisition into

private life, has paved the way for a novel such as is foreshadowed in " Ave." We are a shy people in Ireland now, and Mr. Moore's revelations affected us to hissing as the red-hot iron affects the drop of water. It was not always so with us ; when we were an independent people our social frankness was a terror, and our invective hot as the hob of hell.

This personality of ours that we have tailored so carefully in tradition and prejudice in order that it may appear with fashion and credit amongst the figures of our world—is all in outcry against the rude unrobing of writers such as Mr. Moore. But let us be honest. Does not this outcry perhaps mean that we fear a deeper inquisition and the dragging into publicity of things in our nature that might not posture so well in the limelight as that carefully garbed and tutored figure by whom we desire to be represented, an inquisition that foreshadows that Dread Day when the secrets of all hearts shall be made manifest ? I think when we go profoundly into ourselves, behind this masking personality, we are confronted with a franker being who desires that all barriers shall be broken down ; who realises the oneness of human life, and that our lives are continued in the lives of others ; one who is weary to death of the elaboration of our concealments from one another and who would have all things known, even the worst. What is there to be afraid of after all in the common humanity we share ? Mr. Moore has perhaps encountered this being in himself, and has some inkling of this truth, but with a perversity usual to him he seems to seek truth not for purposes of soul but for purposes of art. I sometimes think Mr. Moore knows very well what he is about, and how wrong is the motive of his inquisition into other lives, and that a consciousness of wrong doing makes him unscrupulous in the uses to which he puts his knowledge.

Mr. Moore should have called his Trilogy " George Moore—A Novel of Contemporary Life," for it is a work of fiction improvised upon his friends and himself. That it is exceedingly well done will not console those who have gained through it an immortality they never coveted. Perhaps there is but one portrait in the books that most people in Dublin will acknowledge to be a genuine one, and that is the portrait of John Eglinton. Mr. Moore has painted him with great skill, real comprehension and kindliness. To " Æ " he has been more than kind, furnishing one who makes no claim to saintship with a halo he has no use for. " Æ " is reported to have said to him : " Moore, you have a passionate literary affection for me, but it is the affection of a porcupine, unconscious of its quills, rubbing itself against the bare legs of a child.".

Mr. Moore has been most flagrantly unjust in his portrait of Douglas Hyde, painting the outer man indeed with a merciless fidelity but totally uncomprehending of the real Hyde. It is a portrait that cries aloud for vengeance on the painter. When " Æ " told Mr. Moore that his portrait of Hyde was glaringly unfair, he replied that it was a case of Jekyll and Hyde, he had painted Hyde and Jekyll was coming on. But Jekyll never came on. I am inclined to think that an incompatibility of temperament between the two types of Connaught men accounts for Mr. Moore's malevolence about Douglas Hyde, all the nausea of " Parnell and His Island " surges up again in his onslaught on him. How indignant one feels at the base caricature of one whose name in Ireland is beloved beyond most names ; the man who drew out of the gutter where we ourselves had flung her, the language of our country, and set a crown upon her ; who by sheer force of personality created the movement in Ireland for the revival of Gaelic, blowing with a hot enthusiasm on that dying spark of nationhood and recalling it to life. Those who know " The Love Songs of Connacht " will not need to be told that here was the soul of a poet. The movement he blasted out of the rock of

Anglo-Irish prejudice in his epic. I wonder how many people realise to-day in Ireland what it meant to give back to the Gael his language; how the honour Hyde put upon the language and the literature straightened the back of young Ireland and interpenetrated all its thoughts. I am prepared to be told, with that curious desire to depreciate that is common to my countrymen, that the Gaelic revival in Ireland was really the work of some bookworm or obscure grammarian. There are always little persons to be found in Dublin grubbing in darkness that they may undermine some reputation, but Douglas Hyde is safe in Ireland. We who remember those days know what Ireland owes to Hyde's fiery spirit, his immense courage, his scholarship, his genius for organisation, his sincerity, his eloquence, and the kindness of his heart.

As to Mr. Moore's little parable of Bouvard and Pecuchet. How ungrateful he is to Pecuchet, for he must often have watched Mr. Gill with half-closed eyes as a cat watches a saucer of cream, dreaming of the copy he should lap up by and by. Mr. Gill was a ready-made Pecuchet, and how well Mr. Moore knew him. He had to find his Bouvard, and he selected Sir Horace Plunkett, whom he did not know at all, for the part. Mr. Moore's comic repentance of this caricature I have already described. Few

people know Sir Horace Plunkett; though
he is the most approachable of men, he is
reserved as only your frank Irishman can
be. His portrait presents many difficulties,
for I might say with perfect truth that he is
a statesman, a large-minded, clear-thinking,
most witty and most courteous gentleman,
and I should not have conveyed any worthy
picture of him or one at all equal to that
which springs up in the minds of his friends
at the mention of his name. He stands, I
think, this unassuming figure, for something
that shall be more intimately of the future
spirit of our country than any shouting
shibboleth of to-day. That one who is so
typically an Irishman in the individualism
of his thinking should be little understood
in his own country is not perhaps very
wonderful. In Ireland we are accustomed
to see a man's mind obliterated in the
movement with which it is identified, and
that Sir Horace has not so obliterated his
mind somewhat disconcerts us. Much has
been written of him in praise and blame,
and I see no reason why I should not sum
up the view he presents to my mind. I see
him as a man who does his own thinking,
excluding no one's opinions, however extreme, but considering all ideas that are
presented to him with a mind dispassionate,
but never cold. His judgment is never
clouded by temper, and one can always

trust him absolutely in every circumstance to take the noble point of view. He is gifted also in a way that is not perhaps generally realised with a wit that bites like mustard, and gets home to its mark as unerringly as the arrow of William Tell.

XII

I HAVE some right, I think, to speak of
Dublin at the time of Mr. Moore's advent,
for I was living here myself, and I was ac-
quainted with many of the dramatis personæ
amongst whom Mr. Moore was shortly to
distribute their parts. I can thoroughly
realise the feeling of Mr. Moore, who, living
in London, had smelt out the pie that was
being made in Dublin and felt that he
himself was one of the ingredients that must
not be missing. I, too, had my feelings in
the matter of pies. When I was a young
girl in Dublin I lived next door to the family
of Purser, and Miss Sarah Purser, then as
now the wittiest woman in Dublin, was the
heroine of my girlish imagination. I felt
I had no talents to equal me to such people,
but I had a singing voice and through it I
would claim my right to be among them.
Many a time have I sat on the stairs at the
top of the house singing away my whole
soul that it might reach them through the
wall and prove that title to be their equal
that the music in me claimed. Many a
year it took me before I got any real share
of their pie, and therefore I cannot help

admiring the daring with which Mr. Moore at once dashed for Ireland and secured his portion.

There was something pathetic in Mr. Moore's return to his native land. Her son who had made himself famous in France and England returning to build up her fortune with his fame and to swagger a little becomingly in his benevolence. And Dublin—Dublin who cares for none of Ireland's sons famous or infamous, except those who stand her drinks—killed no fatted calf for her prodigal, never even knew of his return; worse still, never even knew he had been away. But Mr. Moore, who had mined for himself out of his own reluctant bowels a career and a fame, was not to be daunted by any neglect or contempt in Dublin from shouldering his way in and arranging his pieces on a stage of his own making.

In those first years of the century it seemed to us in Ireland as if not only were our own geese, beloved and wild, returning to us, but tame geese, not our own, were flocking hither also. A queen of England who had not set foot in our island for a generation, led the fashion. One who when she was young and girded herself, walking whither she would, walked not hither; but who, when she was old, and another girded her, bringing her whither she would not, was borne amongst us. And many English people at that time were displaying on their family trees before admiring circles, Irish grand-mothers who had hitherto shared the cup-board with other family skeletons. The English are a simple folk and one cannot be hard upon them. On such simple lines the gods build up great nations.

Dublin at the time Mr. Moore came here was a very pleasant place to live in. It had all the ingredients of an agreeable literary society and a number of persons interested in art or literature or humanity either lived here or made the city frequent visits. George Moore said of Dublin that its " acoustic properties were perfect," so that no jest, be it whispered ever so softly in the closet, fails to be heard on the remotest house-top. It is an ideal home for clever talkers. John Butler Yeats uprooted his family from London where they had been settled for some years and returned here to live. In his studio in Stephen's Green he painted and talked all day long. Mr. Yeats brought his two daughters, distinguished in mind as are all the Yeats family, sharing with their father the gift—made memorable by him in his portraits of women—of dis-covering beautiful and lovable character-istics in their friends. John Butler Yeats had the rare quality that he not only made his women pretty, any artist can do tha , but he made them lovable, manifesting some interior beauty in their souls. Incomparable executants like Sargent and William Orpen have not this faculty ; they exhibit all a woman's character, but no spiritual life looks out of the faces that are so superbly drawn. Nathaniel Hone lived here, the last survivor of the Barbizon School, an old associate of Corot and Millet, full of reminiscences of famous men who seem to us to belong to the classical history of art and himself the most distinguished landscape painter Ireland ever produced, with a massive power of building up the architecture of a landscape, which is rare even amongst the greatest painters. Another attractive personality in Dublin at that time was Walter Osborne, the artist, a most competent craftsman, a charming companion and lovable man whose early death was a great loss to Ireland. John Hughes lived in Dublin then, a sculptor of real talent and still more attractive by his personality, capable of pungent remarks, absolutely free in his mind. Unfortunately for himself he drew upon him Mr. Moore's voracious literary eye, and he made him the Rodney of " The Untilled Field." I do not know whether it is due to this exploitation of his personality that Mr. Hughes decided to live in Paris evermore. William Orpen was also a frequent visitor to Dublin, as free as John

Hughes in his mind and the most devoted slave of the brush that ever came out of Ireland. While here he painted one of the innumerable portraits of the subject of this monogram. His slavery to his tools no doubt made him the master of his art that he is at present. Sometimes Jack Yeats came here, whimsical and kindly, most winning of all the Yeats ; turning by his genius peasants, farmers, tinkers, and the monstrosities of the shows into symbolic images. That nothing might be lacking in the attractiveness of the city of Dublin to a man of Moore's temperament, there flashed across it the most brilliant connoisseur of modern times, the generous, public-spirited, ever-to-be-lamented Sir Hugh Lane.

Mr. Moore's younger brother, Colonel Maurice Moore, often visited Dublin in those days. He has a great deal of the family literary talent and a power of pungent speech which shows that if he had not been a soldier he might have attained a considerable reputation as a writer. Mr. Moore has painted his brother skilfully and mercilessly in the Trilogy, it might not be seemly for one brother to retort on the other by a counter portrait, but as far as insight into character is concerned, Maurice Moore rather than myself should have been chosen to write this epilogue on George Moore's literary

career. For those who know Colonel Moore
only through the pages of the Trilogy it
may be well to state, on George Moore's
private admission, to which we have already
referred, that Maurice has always behaved
like a gentleman. But Maurice Moore is
more than that. He is a distinguished soldier
who was the chief military organiser of the
National Volunteers, a force which Sir
Matthew Nathan states attained a member-
ship of 160,000. He is a good Irishman,
with the fixed principles which are more
readily appreciated by the public than the
fluent ones possessed by his brother George.
An artist who takes or drops his principles
on their literary value is very disconcerting
to the ordinary citizen. It is certainly dis-
composing to find a man who a year ago
was enthusiastic about some idea turning a
cold shoulder upon it because it has served
his purpose as an artist and there is no more
copy in it. Maurice Moore's principles were
not those of an artist but those of a patriot.
From the very fine book he wrote about his
father we gather that Colonel Maurice Moore
inherits from him that public honesty which
was, I think, George Henry Moore's greatest
gift to the politics of his generation. George
Henry Moore possessed a fine honesty and
frankness which he bequeathed to his sons
—the honesty to Maurice, the frankness to
George.

Douglas Hyde, whose eloquent tongue could coax the Gaelic off the bushes, was continually here, the brain and will of the Gaelic League. There were Lady Gregory and William Butler Yeats, an Orpheus who drew that Eurydice out of the Hades of Irish landlordism—strange that his music should also have attracted so unlikely a ghost as Mr. Moore.

Professor Mahaffy lived here. When Mr. Moore came first to Dublin he was inveigled by a fierce environment of Gaels into an attack on Professor Mahaffy, which he bitterly regretted a short time after it was made on hearing that Professor Mahaffy had once said that "Catholicism was essentially the religion of the lower classes." "What a friend he would have been," said Mr. Moore. Professor Tyrrell, with a wit polished in the classic manner, lived here; and there was also Professor Edward Dowden, an excellent critic of literature which had become a classic, but, like most critics a rather more dubious commentator on his contemporaries; a really distinguished mind but without much sympathy for intellectual revivals in his own country. They seemed to him revolutionary, and he compared his attitude to them to Burke's attitude to the French Revolution, and seemed rather to take a pride in acknowledging that he was the solitary Irish

intellectual on the side of the stupid
people.

Edward Martyn was frequently in Dublin
then, interested in all that made for beauty
in his country. His cousin George Moore,
in the Trilogy has fashioned him into a sort
of scapegoat for his own personal antipathies, castigating him for sins he never
sinned. The real Martyn, who hates a
draught as he hates the devil, held his
ground bluffly against all the ill-winds that
cousinly venom could direct against him,
using the consolations of a religion he had
fashioned for himself out of music and the
drama. He comes out of the adversity of
the Trilogy triumphantly ; a figure whom
one regards with affection. " Dear Edward "
was clever enough to deprive George Moore
of the triumph of knowing what his victim
thought of his own portrait, for he steadily
refused to read the Trilogy, saying : " George
is a pleasant fellow to meet, and if I read the
book I might not be able to meet him again."
" Dear Edward " is dear to his friends, not
as he is dear to the malicious literary affection of Mr. Moore, but for his straightfor-
ward and honest humanity, and in spite of
Mr. Moore's malicious portrait, I am certain
there is no one living for whom he has so
sincere an affection as for Edward Martyn.
Mr. Moore has always bestowed his respect
on those who have the courage to disagree

with him, and anybody who has seen Mr.
Moore on the war trail for a scalp knows it
requires uncommon courage to do so. Sir
Horace Plunkett was in Dublin at that
time, the puzzle of the politicians, none of
whom have any politics at all but supply
this deficiency on the one side by prejudices,
on the other by public-houses. There was
also Mr. Rolleston, who should have been a
scholar but for his entanglement in an
economic movement; with an elasticity of
temperament which caused him at his first
contact with Irish Nationality to bound into
Fenianism and from thence to rebound into
an Imperialism that carried him across the
sea to become permanently an Englishman.
Yet I feel that the man who gave us the
beautiful words of a poem like "The Dead
at Clonmacnoise," pervading it with the
honey breath of midland Ireland, deserved
more than the punctured Messiahship accorded him by Mr. Moore. "Æ" was here
—whom reviewers in continually increasing
numbers charge with being a poet, a painter,
and an economist, tracing his career from
the Esplanade at Bray, where he preached
the Ancient Gods of Ireland, through the
counting-house to the bicycle whereon he
roamed Ireland organising co-operative
societies, and into the editorial chair of the
Irish Homestead; but who, in spite of this
weight of evidence against him, remains a

friendly human being who loves a laugh
even at his own expense, and who would be
surprised and probably annoyed if he knew
that there are some who believe that in
Ireland all roads lead to " Æ " ! William
Butler Yeats came here, a poet with a more
exquisite craft in the use of words than any
living poet, and—the noblest figure of them
all—a solitary, unconcerned with any movement, but himself an incarnation of the soul
of Ireland—Standish O'Grady. A name
almost unknown across the Channel, and
often confused with his cousin Standish
Hayes O'Grady, the Gaelic scholar. In the
" Bardic History of Ireland," he opened
with a heroic gesture the doors which revealed to us in Ireland the giant brood of
the Red Branch Knights and the Fianna.
Though a prose writer, he may be called
the last of the bards, a true comrade of
Homer.

Every now and then Synge would loom
up here, saying little and obviously not at
home in cities and much more a companion
of the Arran peasant than of the Dublin
literary folk.

Among other literary persons there were
John Eglinton, so affectionately referred to
in the Trilogy; Richard Irvine Best, who
turned from an original love of Pater and
Wilde and other decadent exquisites to
become a genuine scholar and editor of

ancient Irish texts; Oliver Gogarty, who had but just nipped the wires of the champagne of his wit and sprayed a pungent froth around him.

The infinite variety of Dublin life brought also a dramatic interest which must be dear to an actor such as Mr. Moore. This interest in the theatre brought him into contact with Frank Fay, who had invented a method of teaching actors to speak beautifully, an art which the Abbey Theatre has not yet lost, and his brother Willie Fay, an actor comparable in his own range to a James Welch, who made a most perfect study of "The Playboy of the Western World" and who could—such was his strangely compounded character—have explained to you the ethics of Epictetus or the esoteric significance of the memoirs of the Comte de Gabalis.

At a further period of Mr. Moore's stay in Dublin Seumas O'Sullivan, Padraic Colum, and later on James Stephens, began to be prominent, and one cannot pass from this company without mentioning Mr. Commissioner Bailey, clever, discriminating, at whose hospitable house anything that painted, sang, composed, or acted was sure of a welcome.

With all these colours on his palette, Mr. Moore in the end selected for his picture the most permanent tints, dipping his

brush often in the luscious human com-
pound of T. P. Gill; W. B. Yeats, and " Æ,"
attracted by their brilliant colouring, while
his brother Maurice supplied the sombre
tones.

XIII

ALL these diverse persons were to be found
in Dublin, for the most part hating each
other like poison, but shortly " cross as an
armful of cats," and with or without their
consent to be drawn together in Mr. Moore's
all-embracing literary affection. To a
novelist a society such as this Irish one was
infinitely attractive. In Ireland humanity
develops in its natural forms, it is like
virgin forest, untamed, untrained, uncivilised,
there has been no settled social order to
constrain its growth. The difference between society in England and Ireland seems
to me to be as the difference between wild
forest and forest scientifically planted by a
state forester. The English novelists since
Dickens days have to grub very far below
surfaces to find any differentiation in their
characters. The tall, clean, well-set-up
" God's Englishman " has become a national
ideal. Irish Society has no such minted
ideal and it is unlucky in its false coinage,
aping with equal unhappiness what is un-
real in English as well as in Irish character.
The natural Irishman is then an orgy of
temperament, very often a delightful being,

because—Mr. Bernard Shaw must pardon me—I think a choicer portion of wits fell to this small island than to its more roomy companion, though the culture that has been a good friend to our companion, we to our great hurt have scorned. It is not unlikely that it is the consciousness of untrammelled temperament that makes an Irishman so desirous of that pigeonhole retreat for his soul to which I have referred in another chapter, so unhappy when he has found it, and so confident that it is good for all other Irishmen and so determined to place them there.

At the time of Mr. Moore's return to Dublin some of the group of intellectuals whom I have described were gravitating towards the drama. The story of the intellectual revival in drama in Ireland has been told so often and with such canonical authority that to begin to disentangle truth from falsehood now would be a thankless task and one outside the scope of this book. It is sufficient for my purpose here that I give the honour of the inception of the idea of a school of Irish actors where the honour is due, to the brothers Frank and William Fay. While Mr. Yeats, not himself naturally a dramatist, turned the thoughts of most of his literary contemporaries in Ireland into the writing of plays, the Fay brothers were the avatars of a new creed in Irish acting.

They laboured at their uncommon task each evening when the common labour of the day was done, Frank with his passion for beauty in speech instructing his disciples, young men and women workers such as he himself, and Willie, holding the little company together by his genius as an actor. Not yet, however, had the temple been built that, like so many other fanes, should smother the religion it sought to shelter, and Yeats' " Countess Cathleen " had to content itself with English actors, and when the dual play, Yeats' and Moore's " Dermiud and Grania " was evolved, the Benson company presented it on the boards in Dublin.

The writing of this play was in itself a play. The conjunction of such planetary bodies as Yeats and Moore, who should have been by nature always in opposition, was a portent in the literary heaven. Our Yeats, curved and spiral, a Celtic wonder in mind, at home in the magical regions of Tirnanoge —where are land and water, sowing and reaping but as the heart desires them—and Moore, the bantling of Mayo and Montmartre, concerning himself too often with what Saintsbury calls the " fie-fie " side of the naturalism whose by-product he was. What an alliance ! Literary Dublin sought in the play with intense interest for the footmarks of the writers and when it found God Angus described as " A ragged old man wandering along the mountains prodding a boar," it cried " Lo Yeats " and behold it was Moore, and coming on the description of Conan scratching his head and complaining of lice it said " Lo Moore " and behold it was Yeats. Yeats had come to the collaboration determined to be substantial and material like Moore. Moore had resolved to rise to the heaven of the picturesque and beautiful to meet Yeats. They had passed each other on the journey. The lice came out of Mr. Yeats' fancy and the *Sidhe* out of Mr. Moore's.

Mr. Moore was ever a hero-worshipper, and when Yeats, during the writing of the play, made such strange suggestions as that the first act should be horizontal, the second perpendicular, and the third circular, Mr. Moore was puzzled, but reverent. Walking under his apple trees in Ely Place he cogitated. " The first act—Grania, the nurse, etc. Is that horizontal ? Yes, surely that must be horizontal." Going on to the second act, the question, " What is perpendicular in drama ? " struck a dumb note in his mind, and that mind failed altogether when he came to consider the circular in relation to the third act. This story and the fact that he. accepted from Mr. Yeats a list of words that must not be used because they had been used in literature too much already, and that he even contemplated writing his part of the play in French, Lady Gregory to translate it into English for Yeats to work on, show in a man so full of vanity and egoism as Mr. Moore an extraordinary power of abasing himself before one whom he regarded as a master in the guild of literature. We can never be quite certain that this worship was altogether genuine. We continually find in Mr. Moore a desire to lose himself in some worship. In Mr. Yeats, in Gaelic, in Protestantism, but we always suspect that at the back of his mind he was well aware that he could never unfasten himself from his own moorings and that he had always this feeling, " If I cannot lose myself I shall at least not lose art, and in the end it all produces copy." The story of the spoliation of Edward Martyn in " The Bending of the Bough " has been told with absolute frankness by Mr. Moore in the Trilogy. I should have more confidence in the shame for the theft that he expresses there if he had not used the shame as he uses every asset of emotion he possesses for literary purposes. Edward Martyn's genuine dramatic talent proved in " The Heather Field " was a temptation to a born literary bandit like Mr. Moore, who prides himself on yielding to temptation, and in alliance with Mr. Yeats, always an unfortunate conjunction, Edward Martyn's play was tortured from its original intention and became no play at all, but a dramatic experiment doomed to failure. Mr. Moore would fain have captured also Miss Alice Milligan's "Last Feast of the Fianna," but she defended it "like a little white Persian cat spitting at him from the corner," as he himself described her ; very wisely trusting to her own talents, her confidence being justified in the result.

After "The Bending of the Bough," Mr. Moore broke up his association with Irish drama and with Mr. Yeats, and looked round for other partners. He came to Ireland with, I think, a sincere belief in the literary potencies implicit in the Gaelic League. He may have cherished a faint ambition to learn the language, but as all his friends tell us it took him many years to acquire any facility even in English, he was no doubt deterred from the more complex tongue of the Gael. But he was willing to learn Gaelic vicariously, through his nephews, and he was very firm in his determination that they should miss none of the accents and elisions of the wiliest speech in Europe. But though he did not learn Irish he felt that Irish had much to learn from him, and he placed at the disposal of the Gaelic League the name and fame and talents of a great English novelist and the best-paid writer upon art of his generation. He wrote "The Untilled Field" that Gaelic Ireland might feel its way into modern literature, and no doubt if he had been more careful of Irish susceptibilities some small seed of naturalism might have fructified in Irish soil, which was not unkindly just then to the reception of new influences. He had lived too long out of Ireland to realise that a Gaelic public has the tenderest toes. It has in fact cultivated its susceptibilities into a fine art, believing that its salvation lay in them; Moore's lightest footstep produced anguish. Causes in Ireland are strange creatures, tender and fierce; many of them die in childhood or perhaps the world might harden them. The Gaelic League, an adorable cause for an Irishman, has not escaped this touchiness. Had it not possessed a leader who like Douglas Hyde knew no fear, it too had died in infancy. But his splendid courage swung it through the perils of infancy and adolescence; the pity is that in its most freakish age it developed an ill-timed and ill-directed boldness and dispensed with the leadership of a man of genius in whom lay its only hope of capturing all Ireland. I sometimes wonder if anything now remains for what was, without question, at one time one of the biggest possibilities in Irish life, but a gradual sinking back into that academic stage which in a language precedes decay and death. In Ireland more perhaps than in other places, a movement needs a man. " The Untilled Field " even in a Gaelic translation did not capture Gaelic Ireland. Though there was something in its mood that might have tempted Gaels, I am not surprised at its failure. Mr. Moore's meat for babes contained some elements that might have taxed stomachs inured to stronger diet than any Gaelic Leaguer ever encountered. So like another of his name, " There was trouble on George, Ireland would not do his business for him," and the Gaelic League, like others of his Irish aspirations, went into the melting pot of the Trilogy.

XIV

MR. MOORE after this, I think, rested from movements and became in more than one sense in Dublin a society entertainer. There has always been in him a trace of the Donnybrook Fair Irishman and in his relations with society in Dublin these characteristics frequently appear. The following episode of the green hall door illustrates this : There are certain people in Dublin the desire to shock whom must have been irresistible to one of Mr. Moore's temperament, for Dublin has other and more inexcusable susceptibilities than those of Gaelic Leaguers. There are respectable Irish people who have a morbid horror of anything they consider "unsound" either in religion or politics. These persons are often, though by no means always, our Protestants and Tories, who could better pardon open immoralities than the "unsoundness" I speak of. I feel quite sure that these persons thought Mr. Moore a very bad man, but they might have winked at his badness alone —robust virtue is ever tender to robust vice—but there was an element in Mr. Moore's badness which made it unpardonable in the eyes of true blue Protestant Tories —he truckled with Fenianism. The more a movement in Ireland proclaims itself non-political and non-sectarian, the more your true blue of every section suspects it. To be a Gaelic Leaguer was to be a Fenian, and when such a one painted his hall door in the Fenian colour green, what was this but an open flaunting of his abominable sympathies in a respectable neighbourhood. All Ely Place rebelled, letters were written by neighbours to his landlord. The occasion was one after his own heart and Mr. Moore rushed into the fray with a letter to his landlord, which, I am told, ran somewhat as follows : Mr. Moore said he was glad his neighbours had complained first about him because he had grave complaints to make of their conduct, only being a peaceable man he did not wish to say anything; but now that they had begun the attack, he would say that his neighbours did not clean their chimneys and that large smuts the size of sixpenny pieces floated through his windows and on to his clean doorstep. His neighbours also kept dogs which they beat with sticks, and these dogs howled, which was distressing to a man of humane feelings. The young ladies, his neighbours, were noisy persons who rode their bicycles round and round before his door, ringing their bells and looking at his hall door, which they objected to, and into his windows, which he objected

to. But he would let that pass and come to
the matter of the hall door. He would like
to remind his landlord that he was George
Moore, whose opinion on matters of taste
was more highly paid than that of any other
person in these islands, and he was not
accustomed to find his opinion on such
matters disputed. But he would let that
pass also ; he was a peaceable person and
was willing to agree on a new colour for the
hall door after mutual consultation. But
he would like to remind them that the green
hall door was the key-note of the melody
of colour in the whole house, and the colour
prepared one for the harmonies which un-
folded room by room. As his landlord was
a practical business man he would know that
such harmonies were expensive things, but
still for the sake of peace he was prepared
to evolve a fresh harmony on a new key-
note, the landlord of course bearing the
expense. He did not know which of his
neighbours had made the complaint, so he
was sending copies of the letter to all, and
if they were not satisfied he would write to
the Press and ask the public to judge between
his green hall door and the dirty white of the
hall doors of his neighbours. Mr. Moore's invitation was not, as we may imagine, accepted
—and his hall door remained an oasis of tender green in the desert of Ely Place.

On another occasion, to which I have

referred in an earlier chapter, Mr. Moore's
cook served him with an unsuccessful omelette. Mr. Moore had often explained to his
friends that his tastes in food were very
simple, that just as Whistler had narrowed
down his colours to a couple of tones, so he
had narrowed down his carnal appetites to
a couple of dishes—an omelette—but it
must be properly made, a chop—but it
must be properly cooked. Six cooks within
a fortnight failed to minister to this modest
appetite, and Mr. Moore's indignation in all
probability rose higher and higher at suc-
cessive failures, till it came to pass that the
last of the six went out to get a policeman to
protect her from a flood of artistic expos-
tulation with her cooking wherewith Mr.
Moore threatened to engulf her. Mr. Moore
met the policeman on the doorstep, took
him by the arm and dragged him into the
dining-room, pointed to the omelette and
asked in a tragic voice, "Am I to be compelled by law to eat this?" That his tastes
were really modest is shown by the fact
that the seventh cook proved capable of
evoking from her materials the exact tones
required by Mr. Moore, and she remained
with him ten or twelve years. There is a
distinction between flavours, and as Walter
Pater, Mr. Moore's ancient master in the
art of writing, says, "To miss the sense of
distinction is to miss success in life."

The conversion of George Moore to religion
was an event which interested the Dublin
that goes to the Abbey Theatre and enjoys
good acting and literary art, for the conversion was conceived in the mood of light
comedy. It was reported that the ecclesi-
astical authorities at Maynooth, on the
occasion of the late King's visit there,
decorated that seat of divinity with the
King's racing colours. This may or may not
have been so, but at the moment the account
appeared, religion came to George Moore.
His conversion was as instantaneous as
St. Paul's, and no doubt his experiences en-
abled him later on to understand the Apostle
who is the hero of "The Brook Kerith."
It is possible that the light which fell from
Heaven on Moore was in the nature of a
literary inspiration, and he saw as in a
vision the book which he, a Messiah, should
write about an Apostle. "Ave, Salve and
Vale" occupied him at the moment and it
was needful that "The Brook Kerith"
should be postponed for a few years. But
the wise *litterateur* while working at one
book will prepare his life for the next and
will be collecting experiences. So George
Moore as a prologue to the comedy of his
religion, at once wrote to the papers and
announced his intended reception into the
Protestant communion as a protest against
the decoration of Maynooth with King

Edward's racing colours. The chorus in Dublin, in a mood rightly related to the mind of the protagonist, commented gaily upon the spiritual state of one whose protest against a King took the surprising form of adopting the religion of that King against whom he protested. Mr. Moore desired complete initiation into the mysteries of his new faith. He had his revelation, but revelation has to be reconciled to human reason, and so he went to the Archbishop of Dublin demanding as candidate the rites of initiation. The Archbishop was wiser than he looked, and referred Mr. Moore to the rector of his parish, and so probably escaped an immortality, which I am certain he would not have desired, in the pages of the Trilogy. The Archbishop made the escape of his life, for it was suggested by the chorus that Mr. Moore was trying to kill two birds with the one stone. He hoped to destroy one religion by explaining his reasons for leaving it and another by explaining his reasons for joining it.

His preference for Protestantism was based on the belief that Protestant clergymen were men of the world. This view he explained to " Æ," who expostulated with him for carrying his joke too far, and who said Moore would hurt the feelings of men who were really sincere and pious. " Oh no, ' Æ,' you don't understand ; these men are men of the world." "But I tell you, Moore, that I know many of these men and they are truly sincere and believe what they preach, and they will ask you to pray, Moore, to go down on your knees, Moore, things you have never done in your life, and you will feel very much out of place." "Oh no, ' Æ,' you don't understand ; these are men of the world, they understand perfectly." " Well, I warn you," said " Æ," and departed. After a week had elapsed " Æ " met Mr. Moore and asked him about the initiation. " Well," said Moore, " what you said nearly burst up the whole thing. When the clergyman came I did not wish to appear to be taken in too easily and I worked up a few remaining scruples, fenced for a while and finally announced my scruples as conquered, and myself ready to be received into the fold. Then the clergyman said, ' Let us have a prayer,' and I remembered your words and saw your face looking at me and I burst out laughing. When I saw the horrified look in the clergyman's face I realised it was all up unless I could convince him that it was hysteria, and I clasped my hands together and said, ' Oh, you don't realise how strange all this appears to me to be. I feel like a little child that has lost its way on a long road and at last sees its father,' and I, folding my hands anew, began ' Our Father.' I took the wind out of his sails that way, for he had to join in, but he got in two little prayers on his own account afterwards, and very nice little prayers they were too."

This little child in religion had the enthusiasm of the newly converted. He has told us how he began to read the Bible for the first time, and he went so far as to read the Lessons in a country church in England where he was on a visit. "I believe in Protestantism," he said to "Æ," "I don't mind what anybody thinks." Then he added, looking slyly at "Æ," as an afterthought : "I don't think I could go on reading the Lessons if Mallock came into the church."

When Ireland was rent in two over the prospect of Home Rule, Mr. Moore trailed not a red herring, but a rarer fish across its path when he informed his country, through the contentious columns of the *Irish Times*, that in the restaurant of one Henri in Paris he had eaten a grey mullet. The bones of that mullet, to be sure, stuck in Ireland's throat, but it was still articulate enough to talk, and for days every shade of religion and politics in the country told the *Irish Times* what it thought of mullet and how often it had eaten it in every colour from grey to scarlet. Besides the mullet matter, Mr. Moore trailed his coat in letters to the papers on every variety of subject, irrelevant if possible to any event or emotion of the day, and but seldom trailed it in vain. Someone was always found to respond to the invitation, and Dublin waxed merry over the encounters, and learned to like Mr. Moore more in his character of jester than of patriot; so pleasantly did he, like Bottom, put an ass's head upon him and gambol in our walks.

XV

MR. MOORE having written a book in which he said his farewells to Dublin with all the literary skill at his command, could hardly remain here when the book was published. So he, to whom sacrifice had become the chief ceremonial of his religion as an artist, tore himself away from a charming house and a lively company of agreeable friends, exchanging the soft clean airs of Dublin for stuffy Pimlico where is distilled in its crudest form that mixture of hot rubber and petrol fumes that makes all the Londoners know of atmosphere. Mr. Moore's contributions to literature since his return to London have been lamentable. Casual articles in newspapers on such subjects as whistling for taxicabs, politics and barking dogs. I do not, I confess, think much of Mr. Moore's pronouncements on the last subject, and but that I am committed to a statement of Mr. Moore as an Irishman, his preoccupation with this matter would make me suspect him of an English ancestry. I have often been struck by the sensitiveness of elderly military and naval Englishmen in the matter of the dogs' protesting voice. Any barking that is to be done in England they want to do themselves.

In politics Mr. Moore ranges himself naturally with God and the *Daily Mail* on the side of the big battalions, or, as they view it through the larger other end of their mental opera glasses, the side of the small nationalities. Mr. Moore's make-up, however, is not that of the politician, and one is not surprised to find him an echo. The labour of his mind is all on the side of personal expression, and he has none of the intellectual adroitness that enables the politician to identify his own cause with the cause of humanity. Mr. Moore is very clear about his own cause and never hesitates to hustle other causes off the course. He is primitive, indeed, infantile man, as sure of himself as the baby is. He has escaped all that sophistication of altruism wherewith the guardians of our youth so early confound our confidence in ourselves. Masculine character, as it appears to the feminine mind weary with wisdom from its age-long researches, seldom gets beyond the boyhood stage, and our Peter Pans are dear to us, but Mr. Moore has never got beyond babyhood in his character, and few women can have known him long without that desire to slap him that is the normal woman's attitude towards an aggravating baby, let the sentimentalists say what they will.

I do not find Mr. Moore's essays in the Press in England as amusing as his essays here. Your Englishman being a born sentimentalist, like his German forefathers, will accept no statement of life that is not practical. To get a footing in an English paper Mr. Moore was constrained to link himself on to such obvious nuisances as taxi whistling fiends, and barking dogs. Such flinty matters can kindle a spark of rage, but out of them no pleasant glow of humour comes. Ireland, sure of its practicality, and unutterably weary of it, demands continual imaginative statements of life. The colour of a hall door, the juxtaposition of a policeman and an omelette, the mythical flavour of a mythical mullet, mythically eaten in a French restaurant, such things delight us, as a way of escape from the harsh constraint of our practical temperament. Dr. Mahaffy, the Provost of Dublin University, is more concerned that his girl students should not wear pink blouses than that the course of study provided by his college should be of the slightest intellectual advantage to them, and all Dublin is with him in a hearty appreciation of his attitude and does not care a hang for college courses. The merchants of Belfast, owners of as fine businesses as any in the world, were happier running guns illicitly than they ever were in reading bulky balance sheets.

Your Englishman, conscious of his danger on the sentimental side of his nature, is, in common with his Teuton relative, armouring himself on that side more heavily day by day. I need not talk to Irishmen of their danger in following their practical bent, we —and England also—know it very well. Whether we are right in regarding life as a schoolmaster with a rod in pickle for temperament or whether we are wrong, it is perhaps fortunate for literature, and it is certainly luck for the student of Mr. Moore's wayward character, that he never went to school.

Mr. Moore is safely installed in London now, he has his house and furniture, mahogany doors and pictures and all the burdens that man sets himself to accumulate in his passage through time. He has the occasional society of Mr. Tonks and Mr. Steer to whet his appetite for discussion on art. His excursions into print have not, I fancy, afforded him much amusement, for irrelevant as such trifling was in the midst of an agonising war, they were too much in the key of English life to relieve the boredom of a nature such as Mr. Moore's, which loves to strike a discord. I do not feel that Mr. Moore is as at home in the picture in his London life as he was in Dublin. His opera hat fits in there, no doubt, and his bull-in-the-china-shop truthfulness, which he was diplomatic enough to replace in Dublin by

a more subtle and edged sincerity, probably
serves him well in a country where a Bull is
the popular hero. He has also in cold storage
in his nature, like most Anglo-Irish people,
an appreciation of the well-oiled English
mechanism of life. Yet for all this I hardly
think that one who has never written *Finis*
after any chapter in his life has put the last
seal on his Irish Chapter. I am the more
inclined to think this because there were
wafted to us here in Dublin from time to
time scraps of his latest book " The Brook
Kerith," and although he has made a
pilgrimage to the Holy Land since he left
us the tales borne to me bring airs from Ely
Place. Mr. Moore came to Ireland in search
of a Messiah, and though having tried to fit
the part to each of his friends here and
finding they failed him in some essential
characteristic, he cast himself for it, he cannot have been satisfied with his own pre-
sentation of the part, for in " The Brook
Kerith," he starts the quest anew. The
story of the successor to the Messiahship
has not yet leaked out, but Mr. Moore
presents us with an apostle who believes
that the new religion will not succeed unless
it is associated with a language revival ;
and another apostle who talks about style,
pondering over his Epistles to his followers
with a literary anxiety as keen as Mr.
Yeats' ! I believe it was once said of Mr.

Moore by a member of his family that he would end his days as a monk, and it is certainly true that his later writings show the attraction of religion drawing him closer and closer. It seems, however, to be an attraction of repulsion and to consist rather in renunciations than confessions of faith. In Dublin he renounced St. Peter. In "The Brook Kerith" he confesses St. Paul; but doubtless we shall have a renunciation there also. I think Mr. Moore's contention that his family is of Protestant origin must have some truth in it, for he has a good deal of the Protestant protest against faith in any shape or form. So strong is Mr. Moore's protest against all that relates to the See of Peter, that I believe amongst the many endings he proposed for his book he had almost chosen the following : " You know," he is reported to have said to a friend, " the ordinary legend of the martyrdom of St. Paul I discard as invented by a Church who wanted a long background of martyrs to justify any martyrdoms she herself should inflict. I intend to bring St. Paul in his old age to Spain, where he gradually fades away surrounded by his disciples. At the very last he hears once more the Voice he heard on the way to Damascus, and a light penetrates him with a vision of futurity and he sees with horror all that his religion is bringing on the world. He sees the Inquisition in Spain and Maynooth in Ireland, and he dies crying with all the ferocity peculiar to the Pauline nature, " To hell with the Pope ! "

Mr. Moore is too good an artist to disfigure his book with this freakish story, and too much of an imp not to whisper it in some friend's ear with a confidence which has certainly not been misplaced in the perfect acoustic properties of Dublin.

XVI

A MAN who suffered so much for religion as
actually to submit to pray and be prayed
over would not shrink from further sacrifices,
and after " Ave, Salve and Vale " was com-
pleted the idea of writing a story about
St. Paul, in which Moore's own experience
as a propagandist of religion would be in-
valuable, laid hold of him and, as an artist
conscientious about details, he felt he must
go to Palestine as he went to Ireland for
local colour. No doubt not a scrap of
adventure there will be wasted and we will
get it all in some future tale. But he has
told the story of his wanderings to his
friends so fully, that they have got all
the publicity of rumour and we can set
some of them down. At Marseilles Mr.
Moore embarked on the bluest of blue seas.
" With Marseilles," he says, " my quest
really began. When I looked on those
white shores rising behind me out of the
blue water into the twilight, the precipitous
chalk worn and corroded by the wind into
battlements and parapets and towers, re-
minding the beholder of Valhallas builded
by gods that have been—a beautiful phrase

of William Morris. Those phantasmal ghostly shores rising steeply out of the wave with not a blade of grass enchanted me all through the lingering twilight until they faded as the vessel passed out of the bay, and suddenly I realised where I was and whither we were hastening, and I thought, 'I'm afloat for the first time on the Mediterranean, that sea, around whose shores all the old stories sprang up like flowers.'"

Mr. Moore was so enchanted by antique names and classical memories that he raved around the ship to callous fellow passengers. Here was Sicily, where the naughtiest idylls of Theocritus evoked memories he would willingly have discussed with his shrinking companions. In the lands about this inland sea were born the old gods and especially the goddesses, Venus foam bright rising from the waves and floating shorewards in her shell, Europa and the Bull, Proserpine gathering daffodils on the plains of Enna— on all these legends he dilated. But, alas, his intoxication with classical myth fell flat on companions who desired intoxication with whiskey and soda, and were more interested in a volcano in eruption than in George Moore in eruption. Only one fellow passenger, a silent, pleasant, middle-aged man, seemed to listen to Mr. Moore with interest. He did not talk much but kept the conversation going. Who he was, Mr.

Moore did not know or care. He was a
listener, and the art of picturesque conversation did not rust for want of practice. At
Port Said Mr. Moore had to ship for Joppa,
and here he became aware of a sudden in-
crease in respect for himself. He desired
a cabin to himself, for the thought of being
polite to a fellow passenger horrified him,
but a cabin was a difficult thing to get; yet
when he appeared with his silent companion,
he was treated as if he were an Emperor.
All difficulties were smoothed away. Haroun
Alraschid could hardly have passed amid
more obsequious subjects than did George
Moore, wondering at the way people ran
to do him service. The East welcomed a
Messiah from Ireland, what did it all mean?
He was enchanted if puzzled. He tells us
that on the Joppa steamer suddenly looking
into the hold he saw the East in all its sub-
lime rags: turbans and burnouses, long
skirts half silk, half cotton, in divers
colours, sometimes yellow stripes sometimes
blue, and always turbans, with veils floating
down the back, and fastened with coils of black
camel's hair rope round the head. The Syrian
women are unveiled, the Mohammedans all in
black. There were Jews and a rabbi, a
great paunchy, bearded fellow with a nose
like a flag, all thrown together like so many
cattle and sheep, to sleep as best they could
on their own rags, and there were plenty of

these. Every moment a family would pull
out a sack and drag out its hoard of rags,
and then put them back for no reason a
European could understand. The Bedouins
seemed to him to bear the sadness of sun-
light, for nothing, Mr. Moore thinks, is so
sad as the sun, and the sun-sodden Bedouins
seemed to him sadder than any Irish tinker
he had ever seen.

He was rowed ashore at Joppa in a great
galley like a Roman barge, twelve-oared,
two men to an oar, the rowers chanting
their boat songs. He saw Joppa rising steep
from the sea, house after house, stretching
away east and west, beautiful in outline,
like a strung bow, one minaret above all —
an arrow pointing heavenwards. He stepped
from the vessel into the straggling street, for
there is no shore, and lo, a strange cry ! the
symbol of the East appears, a camel, swinging
great boxes of oranges tiered on either side,
walking with a melancholy resignation sur-
passing that of any saint's, long puritanical
lips, callous tufted hide, the anchorite of
the desert, the nonconformist of the four-
footed world ! The donkeys were beautiful,
well fed and would gallop ringing their
bells —all unlike the Irish donkeys, sombre
and obstinate, and only to be moved by a
union of sticks and profanity. Here again
the hotel melted in obsequiousness to George
and his mysterious companion, and so it

was all the way to Jerusalem. Moore was in search of a monastery where his Essene monks in " The Brook Kerith " could be housed and he wanted to ride on an Arab horse. He refused to ride on English ponies. Go to the East to ride on English ponies ! He must have an Arab horse. There were none, only the Arab draught horses, but still the magical influence prevailed. They would send to Damascus for an Arab steed for George ! Never before attended with such ready service, Moore commented on it to his companion, the middle-aged mystery who went with him to Jerusalem. " I do not know who you are," he said, " but they treat me as if I were a king." " My name is Frank Cook," said the mystery, manifesting itself. Alas, it was not the splendour of George Moore's genius which made the East to bow itself before him, but the fact that his companion was the great Cook, the Adept who conjures tours out of the strange places of the earth, whose presence had caused all obstacles to melt.

When Mr. Moore found that Damascus was a long way from Jerusalem and that he would have to wait a week for his Arab horse, he determined to ride anything he could get, and left the choice of horses to the dragoman. And here Nature who, in the words of Whistler, " is creeping up " to art, brought together for this new Don

Quixote all the materials that had been used so successfully for the old. For the dragoman, a gaunt hungry-looking Arab, appeared next day mounted on a lean roan that would not, Mr. Moore says, have reminded him of Rosinante but that it was accompanied by a small bay pony ! Nature had brought all the players together, but she had juggled the parts, giving the dragoman Rosinante and casting George for the part of Sancho Panza. One sighs for the grotesque pencil of Gustave Doré to make a picture of such a party, to show the plump silhouette of Sancho on the little bay ambling along the peaks of Moab. Probably Mr. Moore said to himself, " A Messiah dare not give any opportunities to the caricaturist ; public men, yes, emperors, yes, but Messiahs, never ! " So as he had cast himself for the part of hero, he could not allow nature to divert him from his purpose and start him on the great errand of his life in such ignoble shape. He insisted on returning to the stables and exchanging the little bay pony for the gaunt Arab draught horse, that was to goose-step him relentlessly with military precision to the top of every mountain and the depth of every ravine between Jerusalem and Jericho, till each several bone in George's body shrieked for mercy. He got riding-breeches made of some terrible material such as people might

make sails out of. Those terrible breeches,
those wooden horses, the heat, the insects,
the precipices he had to climb, fainting,
searching along the Jordan and through
Moab and by the Dead Sea for a monastery.
His horse would not trot ; if it was beaten
it kicked ; it would attempt the exploit of
buck-jumping on the edge of precipices. It
conquered its rider. At last after many
monasteries, too unromantic for the purposes of the tale, were visited, on turning
the shoulder of a mountain one was discovered perched half-way up a precipice over
a valley and below was the Brook Kerith !
Moore is not an adept at climbing and he
had been days in the saddle and was sore
in every atom, but religion is a great power,
and at last he climbed to his rock monastery.
He subsided at last crying, " My God, my
bones, my bones ! " So tired was he that
when he saw a woman there among the
monks he did not even enquire what she
was doing there. " You need say no more,"
said a witty woman who listened to George's
account of his fatigues. " If you saw a
woman in a monastery and did not enquire
as to the cause of her presence there, you
were indeed tired." There in some antique
valley in the neighbourhood of Jericho is the
monastery of the Essenes of the Brook
Kerith. To placate the Abbot, George
prayed for the second time in his life, or

pretended to pray, in the rock cell where Elijah was fed by the ravens. We hear rumours of mountain climbing to which, I believe, "Æ," who has had experience of Mr. Moore's capacity as a mountaineer, listens with a sceptical ear, remembering that George Moore could not get a quarter of the way up Slieve Gullion, and he doubts in a hotter climate these ascents of precipices wild and gigantic as those in a Doré landscape. "Æ," I am told, suggests that Mr. Moore's dragoman or his draught horse carried him or pushed him through these wild adventures. As for the rest of the acts and adventures of this apostle, are they not written in "The Brook Kerith"?

XVII

" THE BROOK KERITH " is the story of Jesus
of Nazareth, whom Mr. Moore represents as
a shepherd belonging to a brotherhood of
Essenes living in a great settlement on the
eastern bank of Jordan. Led by his medita-
tions among the mountains where he fed
his flock to believe that nothing should
come between the soul and God, Jesus went
to be baptised of John the Baptist and his
baptism developed in him a fury of desire to
save his people from the tyranny of the
priests. This led him to Jerusalem. On the
charge of threatening to destroy the Temple
there, which was sustained by his actual
eviction of the money-changers by physical
force, and also of attempted blasphemy in
equalling himself to God, he was, by priestly
instigation, crucified by the Romans. Ap-
parently dead, he was removed from the
cross by his devoted friend Joseph of Arimathæa, who placed him in his own new tomb.
Jesus was not dead, and was restored to
health by Esora, Joseph's ancient nurse.
He is taken back by Joseph to the Brook
Kerith, the monastery where his former
brethren the Essenes had settled, and there

he is restored to his task as shepherd of
their flocks. Wandering again among the
hills, he came to healing of his mind, shattered as it has been by his terrible experiences. After many years when Jesus was
coming to himself, Paul the Apostle being
persecuted by the Jews takes refuge at
the Brook Kerith and is there confronted
by Jesus, on the story of whose death and
resurrection he had staked all his hopes and
founded many Christian churches. Paul
refuses to admit to his mind the truth of
Jesus' story and leaves the monastery with
Jesus as his guide to Cæsarea. Paul wraps
firmly round him his belief in his own
Apostleship which had been conferred on
him in vision from a Christ in heaven, and
puts away from him as delusion the real
Jesus and the teaching he would have given
him. Jesus leaves Paul in safety near
Cæsarea, and we have a momentary passage
across the stage of some Buddhist monks,
when Jesus disappears from our view, while
Paul pursues his journey to Cæsarea and
finally to Rome.

The rumours that had reached us in
Dublin of " The Brook Kerith," were many of
them dispersed for me when I read the book
itself. I was reminded for an instant —so
do trivial matters arise uninvited in the
mind during its most serious occupations —
of those suggestions, to which I have referred

before, made by Mr. Yeats to Mr. Moore when together they fashioned the play of " Dermiud and Grania." The first act, Mr. Yeats said, should be " horizontal." Mr. Moore was puzzled at that time by Mr. Yeats' geometrical language, but I think he must have since gone profoundly into this matter, for in " The Brook Kerith " we have a book that might be described as horizontal for the first 442 pages, rising suddenly then into one vertical peak and subsiding at page 466 to the horizontal again and continuing at this level up to its close on page 471.

It is perhaps a tribute to Mr. Moore's power of transporting us to the East where he has laid the scenes of his story, that when one attempts to criticise " The Brook Kerith," one is led into a labyrinth of tropes and images that are more in the nature of eastern than of western literature. I might call " The Brook Kerith " a recital in a musical undertone such as those that beguiled " The Arabian Nights " ; the voice is never raised, the key never altered save in that moment when Paul talks noisily to Jesus on the road to Cæsarea, and then the tones fall again into a murmur. I might say that the book represents a space of time filled with momentous happenings that yet fall silently as the sand in the hour-glass, and for all their meaning, there remains for us in the end but a little mound of sand. Mr. Moore has been at extraordinary pains to hush all sound in the book. " Down, down," he says to every fawning fancy that leaps up to his hand. " To heel, to heel," he says to any passionate emotion that threatens to overleap the bounds he set it. And perhaps he has done wisely. In attempting to retell the story of the Gospels he subjected himself to a tremendous ordeal, and that he has emerged from it with any credit at all, is a high tribute to his art as a writer.

I remember that John Eglinton says in one of his essays that " no one could improve upon the story of David, unless, by a miracle, he could introduce some new and transforming element into his conception of it." He says that " when a great legend or narrative comes down to us from antiquity—as, for instance, the Biblical story of David—it does so in a certain form in which it has spontaneously clothed itself and which fits it as the body fits the soul." The story of the Son of David had behind it more than a thousand years of marvelling worship before our English translators wove it into the amazing literature we know to-day. He who would part such a garment undertakes a terrific task. His tale must inevitably seem to compete with the scripture story — that unequalled epic that begins with the

Birth that is coincident with the birth of a
new star in space, and that goes on, every
line a phrase of music, to tell of Him who
shall lead humanity, sickened with the bitter
fruit of Eden, to the healing tree that springs
up in the street of that Holy City that is
built about the throne of God. Who shall
worthily re-sing that song that note by
note has sung itself into every event of life
and death of centuries of English-speaking
Christians, so that many of us hardly know
now if it is the story, or the manner of its
telling, that enchants us ?

Mr. Moore brings upon his head also the
reproach Plato put upon the poets who
brought the gods into disrepute, making the
heavenly story common, bringing the esoteric teaching of the mysteries down to such
materialistic tales as confront us to-day in
the pages of the classical dictionary.

One opens such a book as " The Brook
Kerith " fearing that the *morbus pediculosis*
that so often afflicts the realistic writer may
leave its unclean trace on the spotless tale
our Bible gave us. But Mr. Moore has been
saved from this horrible ending to his literary
career. It seems to me in reading the book,
that instead of taking the story in his own
hands and carrying it his own way, the story
took him and carried him whither it would.

Joseph of Arimathæa, whose life the
Bible dismisses almost in a phrase, is the

man whose spiritual struggle occupies the greater portion of "The Brook Kerith." If a book so still could be said to have any motion one might divide the tale into three movements. The Joseph movement, slow and languid, which merges into the more solemn movement of the Messiah's story, and the Pauline discord which twangs out noisily before the murmuring close. Joseph of Arimathæa's quest is Mr. Moore's own quest, and one must regret that one who has shown in this book, with an art few writers possess, the passionate desire for worship that starts the human heart on so many restless pilgrimages, should himself seem to be so satisfied that all his own quests shall end in the discovery of a happy phrase. This may be an unjust estimate of Mr. Moore, and it may seem absurd to bring a moral issue into a literary criticism, but I, in common with most women, can only separate the intellectual question from the moral one with extreme difficulty, nor can I follow Mr. Moore in his extraordinary preoccupation with what seems to me the mere scaffolding of life. I may be captured by the happy phrase, but I cannot rest in it with any lasting satisfaction.

I cannot help being consumed with curiosity to know if Mr. Moore altered the purpose of his book as he went on. I had divined a book almost entirely about St.

Paul, and looked forward to a Mr. Moore
who, having failed in works, should justify
himself as St. Paul justified himself, by
faith. But instead of this rugged, hearty
optimist as principal hero I find the lovable, delicate, sceptically-minded Joseph of
Arimathæa who drew his Messiah rather out
of his own warm heart than out of any
profound intellectual adventure. The story
leads one with wonderful skill through
Joseph's many searchings after a prophet
to his meeting with the Galilean Essene.
After the crucifixion and disillusionment of
Jesus, the prop that Joseph gave the story
is cunningly withdrawn, and the way is
prepared by the account of Jesus' absorption
in the daily common task of shepherd on
the hills for the complete self-realisation
that came to him with the dramatic entrance
of Paul. Paul's occupation of the stage is
somewhat violent, but his time there is
brief if noisy, and the book dies away in
silence with his arrival at Rome. I had
imagined a development of the character of
Paul. But Paul's character has no development. It springs on the page fully armed,
and remains there mail-clad and unchanging.
The curtain goes down on Paul's iron-bound
mind.

Mr. Moore has chosen an extraordinary
theme, and that he has been able to raise the
disillusioned, broken prophet into a being

more nearly divine than he who was crucified because he claimed divinity, we must admit to be a great achievement, if we are content to waive the question—a literary as well as a moral question—whether any writer is justified in breaking up the mould of such a story as the Gospel story.

He has given us more than the ravelled thread such an attempt might produce. He has given us an absorbing study in a rare psychology, as well as a complete realisation of a land of milk and honey, of deserts and ravines and lakes, fierce and tender, forbidding, stern and bountiful, a land that could produce a truculent anthropomorphic deity made in the image of its own inhabitants, and yet gave humanity the Divine Shepherd of the Psalms and the compassionate and gracious figure that has allured Christendom for 2000 years.

Mr. Moore has put some of his best writing into "The Brook Kerith." There are beautiful passages that describe Joseph and Azariah roaming in the woods about Arimathæa. The silence of the forest, "if silence it could be called, for when they listened the silence was full of sound, innumerable little sounds, some of which they recognised; but it was not the hum of insects, or the chirp of a bird, or the snapping of a rotten twig that filled Joseph with awe, but something that he could neither see nor hear nor smell nor touch. The life of trees—is that it? he asked himself. A remote and mysterious life was certainly breathing about him and he regretted he was without a sense to apprehend this life."

The meeting between Jesus and Joseph by the Lake of Galilee is related as follows :—

" Joseph could re-see the plain covered with beautiful grasses and flowers, with low flowering bushes waving over dusky headlands, for it was dark when they crossed the plain ; and they had heard rather than seen the rushing stream, bubbling out of the earth making music in the still night. He knew the stream from early childhood, but he had never really known it until he stood with Jesus under the stars by the narrow pathway cut in the shoulder of the hill, whither the way leads to Capernaum, for it was there that Jesus took his hands and said the words ' Our Father which is in Heaven.' At these words their eyes were raised to the skies, and Jesus said : Whoever admires the stars and the flowers finds God in his heart and sees him in his neighbours' face. And . . . he recalled the moment that Jesus turned from him abruptly and passed into the shadow of the hillside that fell across the flowering mead. He heard his footsteps and had listened, repressing the passionate desire to follow him and to say : Having found thee, I can leave thee never again . . . through the myrtle bushes he could hear the streams singing their way down to the lake, and when he came to the lake's edge he heard the warble that came into his ear when he was a little child, which it retained always. He heard it in Egypt under the pyramids, and the cataracts of the Nile were not able to silence it in his ears." . . . " One of those moments when the soul of man seems to break, to yearn for that original unity out of which some sad fate has cast it—a moment when the world seems to be one thing, not several things; the stars and the stream, the colours afloat on the stream, the birds' song and the words of Jesus."

I have made these quotations, though I do not care to make quotations, because they seem to me to convey some idea of the musical undertone in which the book is written. A great deal of it is in prose like the warbling water that Joseph heard. Yet beautiful as much of the book is, is not Mr. Moore in writing it like unto those rational-ising writers who broke up the mould of the old pagan beliefs of Greece and Rome, making indeed a literature but defrauding the world of deity? He puts upon the God-head feet of clay, successor to those who in turn have resolved into a philosophic ration-alism every divine tale that blessed hu-manity.

" The Brook Kerith " is an epilogue to a beautiful story written by a man tired of the theme, yet who cannot invent anything more beautiful than the story he wrecks. He has no faith in any new vision, nothing wherewith to build up a new spiritual romance to make the world breathless with fresh beauty.

XVIII

I HAVE written in this book at some length of Mr. Moore as an Irishman because although he has lived the greater part of his life in England and France, during the years that he lived here his house in Ely Place was a centre in its way for the literary folk in Dublin and his influence is of some account. There has always been a certain sterility in Irish ideals ; we reach for a star or we scramble lower down for a terrestrial bauble. In all their aims high and low Irishmen have a tragical alienation from life. They became peasant proprietors more because their fields were symbolic of the four fields of Kathleen ni Houlihan than because they might be sown and harvested and produce the food of man. They value their municipal privileges more for the sense of power these confer than from any serious intention of using these powers for simple human needs and comforts. Their political power has been treated as a game as diverting as musical chairs at a children's party, sitting, acting and voting to meaningless party tunes played at hazard and stopped at hazard. If this were not so, would we have our land in grass, our towns and cities in slums, and our country without a human hope to break down the barriers that our several quests have imposed upon us ?

Mr. Moore as a man of feeling was no doubt moved by this sterility in Irish ideals, and he attempted almost brutally to introduce a personal and human ideal in Irish literature. His literary theories might in time have justified themselves here, had he not been deflected by his own excessive egoism from any serious attempt on the heart of Ireland. Where he proved himself stupid was in assuming, in his attempt to carry his literary theories into practice, that the life to be expressed here in literature was of the same quality as the life to be expressed in other countries. Humanity in Ireland has never become self-conscious. We are intensely conscious of our nationalism, of our imperialism, our religion, Catholic and Protestant, but beyond these we are the least introspective race in Europe. Mr. Moore's art is self-conscious and introspective, a very complete expression of the humanity to which he was most accustomed. His art went all astray in Ireland. He supposed in us a feverish interest in sex. Ireland regards sex, when she regards it at all, with an entirely primitive and practical eye. Love in Mr. Moore's use of the word she would consider balderdash. She is approach-

able to the literary explorer on the side of
the affections. Friendship and affection
are extremely strong here, but they are not
self-conscious. Mr. Moore, whose nature, as
I have said elsewhere, fits him much more
to write of affection than of passion, might,
had he been patient, truly have served
Irish literature and affected Irish life. His
impatience and perverseness hindered him.
This aspect of Irish life has never had an
interpreter worthy of it, and Mr. Moore
might have been that interpreter. I think
we want an interpreter, and that perhaps
the time has come for one, though it is
difficult for one to realise this who has seen
an Ireland grow more and more obsessed
by the cinema and the penny novelette. The
impossible cracksman of the one and the
impossible duke of the other are both as
far away from life as any legend of Saint
or Sidhe. We are in a sorry plight, whom a
foolish system of education has robbed of
those bardic heroes who should have been
the natural exemplars of our youth. What
room was there in our school primers for the
extravagant Gaelic heart ? Our intellects
were not bred true to type and we have a
mongrel taste. He was a wise man, that
Danish bishop Grundtvig, who reared his
High School pupils on their native hero tales.
The ordered social life of rural Denmark is
the result of that inspiration. Still I cannot

imagine Mr. Moore as the novelist of the Red Branch or the Fianna.

I write this last chapter of my book in a city that has been shattered by the big guns of modern warfare. It is a heavy ending for a book begun with a light heart. With every twenty-five years of Irish life we expect a tragedy, with every fifty years it inevitably comes. Can any ruling country afford to neglect such portents ? Can it be stupid enough to imagine that a nation whose belief in its own high destiny is so profound that seven hundred years of English domination have failed to obliterate it, will ever lose that hope ? One hundred and eighteen years have passed since the last passionate outburst of that hope, and the revolution of 1916 is but begun. The spirit that inspired it is no less fervent than it was then, and is as widely spread in Ireland, for all the protests of our members at Westminster. It may be a town movement now and in alliance with a hungry labour, as it was a country movement then and in alliance with a hungry tenantry. It is the same movement, it possesses hearts as brave and martyrs as willing. One portion of Ireland expresses its desire for freedom of government by constitutional methods and by taking arms to serve England, one by taking arms against England. This desire should appeal to a people like the English who were wont to love freedom themselves and who fought for it so bravely against their kings and nobles ; who wrung from them by insurrection and by civil wars the charters of their constitution. What Englishman but thinks with pride of how the town of York held all England at bay and let its king batter vainly at its gates, till he had yielded it the charter of its civic rights ? Are we to have no charters in Ireland but dishonoured charters, no treaties but broken treaties ? Yet I would be just to England. She is surely in a desperate strait, when within her own borders she is compelled to treat as a " scrap of paper " the most cherished charter of her people's liberties, the Habeas Corpus Act. That she should suspend it here is natural enough, angered as she was at our disaffection and at the timing of our revolution. That she suspended it at home is a bad omen in a country which has grown great through its passion for individual liberty.

It may seem to my readers as if I had shoved Mr. Moore aside in the preceding paragraphs. Surely, they may say, I did not dream that there was any part in our recent tragedy that Mr. Moore might have been cast for. I have not done with Mr. Moore at all, though it was no part of my plan in this book to arraign him or any

absenting Irishman at the bar of his country
and ask him to show cause why he has not
devoted such gifts as were his to her service.
That would be an absurd position for me to
assume; Mr. Moore at the helm in Dublin
during such a storm as has broken here
would be an absurd spectacle. Yet it
should not be unnatural for an Irishman to
be seen in the service of his country. Mr.
Edward Martyn, who has never been a
sentimentalist about Ireland, and who has
indeed given her many shrewd knocks, has
believed himself to have a duty towards
the country whence he draws his income
and has fulfilled that duty. Sir Horace
Plunkett has acknowledged the same obli-
gation; so too has " Æ."

Had Mr. Moore any gifts that he might
have given to Ireland? I believe his frankness might have been of great benefit to
our public life, and his intense concern with
human life and emotion might have im-
parted a warmth to our literature that is
missing from it now. The spirit and the
flesh are very far apart in Ireland. So unnatural a distance is between them that the
conquest of the material by the spiritual,
which is, I suppose, the end of all religion,
promises to be a long and tedious process
here. I remember the sufferings inflicted
on Mr. Edward Martyn by the earthliness
of the feminine soprano in Church music

and how he fought for the aloofness of the boyish treble. He won too, but I think he had done better had he waited for the aloofness of Palestrina to capture the feminine soprano. The separation of the spirit and the flesh, the churches tell us of, will surely be done much more efficiently hereafter than we can do it now. The purpose of our existence here is more properly to bring heaven to earth. Yet Mr. Moore would surely be a most inappropriate prophet of such a creed. Heaven may have cast him for this end, but the rival establishment intervened.

I often wonder what effect upon our normal constitution here in Ireland had all the movement of that febrile time that we call the Irish literary revival. Has any intellectuality at all emerged out of it, any public opinion, any essentially national flavour in our life ? True, some of our educational establishments are aware now of what was then unknown to them, that in Mr. Yeats and " Æ " we have poets of whom any nation should be proud. It can hardly happen now as in those days when one Alexandra College student whispered to another that she had heard by way of a French review that there was a literary movement in Ireland. Yet our public life in Ireland is as barren of thinking as it ever was and there is no true cohesion amongst us, though there are many enforced unities.

There has been no lack of courage in Ireland ; there never is, but even our courage has a fatal quality. Mr. Moore has a moral courage that he has developed to the point where it becomes immorality, as most of his friends realised when they read his " Ave, Salve and Vale." He was content to rear his monument in the Trilogy, and though one may regret that he has not a nobler ambition, it is in a sense an achievement. A century hence people will search in it as eagerly as they search in Hogg and Trelawney for memories of Shelley and Byron. Mr. Yeats and his literary contemporaries in Ireland may have a more kindly, but they never will have a more brilliant, chronicler. Literary history must accord Mr. Moore a place amongst the most brilliant and varied writers of our time. Still, he will be remembered less by the creations of his imagination than for his malicious and witty account of his contemporaries.

In the " Memoirs of My *Dead* Life," he wished that his body after death might be cremated and the ashes enclosed in a Greek vase, with dancing fauns and nymphs modelled around its curves, but it would be far more appropriate to place round the vase which holds his ashes the figures of the Irish literary revival, with George Moore as Pan playing on his pipes the movement of their dance.